ADVANCE PRAISE FOR
ALIGN, EXPAND AND SUCCEED

"Align, Expand and Succeed *speaks volumes about how important it is for entrepreneurs to shift their inner game if they want to experience outer success. I encourage you to read it right away.*"

~T. HARV EKER
AUTHOR OF THE #1 NEW YORK TIMES BEST SELLING BOOK *SECRETS OF THE MILLIONAIRE MIND*

"*This collection of heartfelt stories reveals the wisdom and truth of what it takes to align your career with your soul while inspiring you to get into action in new and rewarding ways.*"

~ARIELLE FORD, AUTHOR OF *THE SOULMATE SECRET*

"*If you want to make a difference in the world through your business, you need to read this book! In these pages, the authors outline powerful strategies that will streamline your goals of using your business as a vessel to both achieve success and to positively impact the world.*"

~DR. IVAN MISNER, NY TIMES BESTSELLING AUTHOR
AND FOUNDER OF BNI AND REFERRAL INSTITUTE

"*This book will help anyone striving to succeed in this new world (and new economy) as a business owner. The future depends on the success of entrepreneurs, and this book gives you both heartfelt inspiration and practical strategies that help.*"

~LORAL LANGEMEIER, CEO/FOUNDER OF LIVE OUT LOUD, INTERNATIONAL SPEAKER AND BEST-SELLING AUTHOR OF THE THREE-BOOK *MILLIONAIRE MAKER* SERIES AND *PUT MORE CASH IN YOUR POCKET*   WWW.LIVEOUTLOUD.COM

"Align, Expand and Succeed *provides soul-vision for entrepreneurs of integrity and heart to integrate into their lives. It's full of inspiration and step-by-step practices you can incorporate for a more successful and aligned business – and life."*
~JUDITH SHERVEN, PH.D. AND JIM SNIECHOWSKI, PH.D.
AUTHORS OF THE #1 BESTSELLER *THE HEART OF MARKETING*

"If you're searching to find a way to be true to who you are while experiencing great success in your business, you've found what you're looking for in this book."
~MILANA LESHINSKY, AUTHOR OF *COACHING MILLIONS*

"Christine, Lynne and the contributors of this book are on the cutting edge of what makes entrepreneurship work today, which is to align with your highest calling in life. This book is a manual for learning how to expand into the world in a powerful way and manifest the success you want and deserve. I highly recommend it… your heart will be full!"
~ROBIN FISHER ROFFER,
AUTHOR OF *THE FEARLESS FISH OUT OF WATER* AND *MAKE A NAME FOR YOURSELF*

"As our world changes, it is imperative that entrepreneurs and leaders operate on a higher level of conscious awareness and empowerment. This book provides the tools and the inspiration to quickly move business people into the next strata, to light the way for greater profitability, spiritually-based business leadership and global contribution."
~JACKIE LAPIN, AUTHOR OF THE NO. l BESTSELLER, *THE ART OF CONSCIOUS CREATION*
AND WORLD LEADER IN PRACTICAL CONSCIOUS CREATION

"Inspiring, powerful, authentic and true. Align, Expand and Succeed *reveals a progressive approach to creating more success for yourself and the world around you... from the inside out. A must read!"*

~ALEXIS MARTIN NEELY, EVOLUTIONARY ENTREPRENEUR,
WWW.ALEXISMARTINNEELY.COM

"Being aligned inside and out is essential for attracting what you desire in your business and your life. Align, Expand and Succeed *provides ample inspiration and information to help you do just that. I highly recommend it."*

~CHRISTY WHITMAN, FOUNDER OF THE QUANTUM SUCCESS COACHING ACADEMY
AND WWW.7ESSENTIALLAWS.COM

"The pages of this book are filled with real stories from entrepreneurs around the world who have committed to 'authenticity in business' and have reaped the abundant rewards! Very inspiring... and essential reading to thrive in our changing world."

~LISA SASEVICH, "QUEEN OF SALES CONVERSION" WWW.LISASASEVICH.COM

"Business is changing at the speed of consciousness and now more than ever, it's vital to get connected with your own vision and purpose, and boldly deliver that message to the world. In Align, Expand and Succeed, *the authors successfully take you step-by-step through the conscious entrepreneur's journey through the eyes of inspiring visionaries who have blazed the trail for you. Read this book and you'll know with absolute certainty that you can achieve anything upon which you focus your vision and consistently take inspired action."*

~JEFFREY HOWARD, CEO AND CHIEF "VISIONEERING" OFFICER,
MASTERMINDMENTOR.COM AND VISIONARY BUSINESS UNIVERSITY

"Align, Expand and Succeed *is a powerful collection of stories by entrepreneurs who are saying YES to helping usher in a new world through their businesses. It's inspiring, touching and deeply impactful. When you read their stories, you may never be the same. In fact, you may become more of who you are meant to be"*

~REV. DR. LORRAINE COHEN, GIFTED SPIRITUAL LIFE COACH, SPEAKER, BROADCASTER, AND CEO, POWERFULL LIVING

"If you're looking for a way to bring consciousness and business together in an integrated, aligned way… look no further than Align, Expand and Succeed. *It offers an abundance of wisdom from entrepreneurs who are walking this path every single day."*

~MAX SIMON, A GLOBAL AUTHORITY FOR TRANSFORMATIONAL BUSINESS EVENTS / GETSELFCENTERED.COM

ALIGN EXPAND *and* SUCCEED

Shifting the Paradigm *of* Entrepreneurial Success

COMPILED BY

CHRISTINE KLOSER & LYNNE KLIPPEL

Love Your Life

LOVE YOUR LIFE PUBLISHING, INC.

Love Your Life Publishing, Inc.
7127 Mexico Road Suite 121
Saint Peters, MO 63376
www.LoveYourLifePublishing.com
publisher@LoveYourLifePublishing.com

ISBN: 978-1-934509-31-9
Library of Congress Control Number: 2010933604

Printed in the United States of America

Cover and Internal Design by: www.Cyanotype.ca
Editing by Marlene Oulton and Gwen Hoffnagle

First Printing: 2010

DEDICATION

This book is dedicated to all entrepreneurs who are purposefully transforming the world by investing their hearts and souls in their businesses. Your integrity, passion, and commitment to serve are inspiring. Like a ripple in a pond, your efforts make a profound difference to your clients and customers… and to our evolving world.

"Thoroughly unprepared,
we take the step into the afternoon of life.
Worse still, we take this step with the
false presupposition that our truths and our ideals
will serve us as hitherto.
But we cannot live the afternoon of life
according to the program of life's morning,
for what was great in the morning
will be little at evening
and what in the morning was true,
at evening will have become a lie."

~ CARL GUSTAV JUNG

TABLE OF CONTENTS

Part Three – Succeed

Foreword

MICHAEL PORT

What does it mean to be an entrepreneur? Does it mean that you are throwing off the shackles of working for a behemoth corporation? Does it mean you finally have an opportunity for full self-expression and creativity in your work? Does it mean that you can control your future and determine your destiny? Does it mean that you can build wealth and security in a way that might not be possible when working for someone else? Maybe it means all of these things to you, or none of them, for that matter. Which is exactly my point. It's up to each of us to decide what it means to be an entrepreneur. To really ask, "Why am I choosing entrepreneurship? What's the point of this choice?" Because the entrepreneurial path can be challenging, to say the least, even for the best and the brightest – even the most experienced and promising among us can succumb to the pressure of owning a business.

One would assume that that these pressures are external: financial, managerial, economic, and the like. And they will be, you can count on it. But the downfall of many unsuccessful entrepreneurs comes not just from external pressures, but also from internal pressures in the form of personal problems.

I believe that many of the problems you will face in your business are, in fact, going to be personal problems in disguise. Not only have I seen this demonstrated among the tens of thousands of business owners with whom I've worked, but I've experienced it myself. Most of us have an unresolved issue or two, or three (or thirty) still floating around our heads. And if you're not careful, these unresolved personal issues may quickly become unresolved business issues.

Are you familiar with the saying, work on your business while working in your business? It's good advice, for sure. I would just add... while working on yourself.

It's so very helpful to understand which of your character traits work for you and which work against you, and then do the personal work to address these "character defects" before they become person problems. You'd be amazed at how fast a personal problem can morph into a business problem that threatens to derail your big plans.

The condition for intellectual capital is big thoughts. The condition for spiritual capital is love. Your future rests on both. And, fortunately, an opportunity for both intellectual and spiritual growth is exactly what this book offers.

An entrepreneur grows a business only to the level at which she can handle that growth from an emotional, spiritual, psychological and intellectual perspective. So, if you increase both your intellectual and spiritual capital, you will expand your capacity to handle bigger problems and achieve bigger goals... more easily.

Ask yourself: "What am I really doing? Am I truly happy in my work? Am I serving in the best way possible? Am I contributing in the way I'm meant to? Is there more than this? And if there is, what is it and how do I find it?

It is exciting to see a book like Align, Expand and Succeed: Shifting the Paradigm of Entrepreneurial Success offer answers to these profound personal questions. If you want to connect deeply with your purpose so you can stand in the service of others as you stand in the service of your destiny, this book, if you let it, can be your muse.

I also like the business models offered in this book. They are collaborative, emotionally conscious, and require social contribution from you as a creator. Moreover, I appreciate the transparency of the book's authors, Christine Kloser and Lynne Klippel. Their personal stories of challenge, struggle, and inner turmoil, coupled with inspiring success and achievement, show their commitment to living truthfully. Their vulnerability and willingness to share these stories with you, in service of your personal and professional growth, is reflective of their generosity and grace.

This book will help you close the gap from where you are today to where you want to be… serving the people you're meant to serve. And I believe that there are certain people you're meant to serve and others that you're not. Your job, if I may be so bold as to suggest, is to do everything in your power to find those people. And only you can share your message. I, for one, would love to hear it. Keep thinking big about who you are and what you offer the world.

Thank you for giving me the opportunity to be of service to you. I love you very much – and not in a weird way – but for standing in the service of others as you stand in the service of your destiny.

Warmly,

Michael Port
New York Times bestselling author of four books
including *Book Yourself Solid* and *The Think Big Manifesto*

Introduction

Thank you for opening the pages of this book. You've just said "yes" to the part of you that yeans for a new way of "being" in your business and your life... the part of you that knows there has to be a better way, and is committed to discovering and living that new way for your own good and the good of our world.

As the compilers and publishers of Align, Expand and Succeed: Shifting the Paradigm of Entrepreneurial Success, it is our deepest intention that this book open that new world for you; a world of inner and outer transformation, a world of joy, ease and success in your business (and your life), and a sense of never feeling alone on your path again.

We assure you there's a growing number of entrepreneurs who are seeking and adopting a new model for their business... one that emerges from the inside out. How do we know? Because as book publishers we keep hearing conversations about this "new" way of being in business; about the changes that are happening in our world, the urgency entrepreneurs feel to do something about it, and their deep desire to share their wisdom with the world.

For us, the best way we know to share wisdom is with the written word... through books. So, we paid attention to the conversations we were hearing and to our belief that books change lives. We decided the best thing we could do to help bring the world into more alignment at this crucial time was to give voice to the conversations we were hearing.

It is in these pages that we do this. What you'll discover as you read this book is that we are all more alike than we are different. We have the same desire for living a purposeful, passionate, fulfilling, meaningful and successful life. Granted, the picture of what that looks like for each of us differs... but the essence is the same.

Compiling this book was our effort and contribution to help your desire for a new world become reality – a world that begins with YOU!

But, in all honesty, our part was easy in bringing together the powerful voices in this book. The contributing authors are the ones who deserve all the credit. You'll see as you read each chapter, that the writers have opened their hearts to you, they have shared their greatest fears and challenges... as well as their greatest victories and successes, both inside and out. They each give you a key to their soul, a key to their success, and a key to unlock places in your soul that are waiting to be touched.

This book is a kaleidoscope of stories that will inspire you, touch you, and empower you to live your life in a more powerful, peaceful, and aware manner. Business is changing. Who you are as a business owner is just as important as the tasks you perform. The old models of fierce competition, profits at all costs, and unethical business practices are falling away. The new paradigm of business, which we call conscious business, focuses on collaboration, authenticity, serving customers with heart, and contributing to the healing of our planet. When you consciously choose to use eco-friendly products, negotiate business deals with impeccable integrity, or focus on solutions that benefit everyone, you are acting as a conscious business person.

That world you dream of, the business you dream of, the impact you dream of having are all there for you. We feel that the treasures awaiting you in this book are the keys for you to discover that world and thrive in it for the rest of your living days.

You can use this book in two different ways. You can read it from cover to cover and absorb the diversity of viewpoints about conscious business.

Or you can browse through the chapters randomly, choosing those that appeal to you the most and reflecting on one message at a time before moving on to the next.

And as you do, keep in mind that this great shift we're all going through in this time and space is not about us who are here now… it is truly about creating a new world for generations to come. We invite you to join us as conscious entrepreneurs, letting your heart and soul guide your business along with your knowledge and expertise. As we all become more awake and conscious of the greater good in our individual business endeavors, we will create a better world.

You are here now because you are needed as part of this shift into a new world. We hope you will heed that call, open your heart to the possibilities that live in these pages and join us in the urgent and exciting journey of raising consciousness on the planet, one entrepreneur at a time.

When you ALIGN with who you truly are, and EXPAND your presence in the world… SUCCESS naturally flows in abundance to you. And this, dear reader, IS the journey of shifting the paradigm of entrepreneurial success.

We are grateful you've chosen to join us by reading this book and connecting with the 39 conscious entrepreneurs who made it possible.

With gratitude,

CHRISTINE KLOSER & LYNNE KLIPPEL
Love Your Life Publishing, Inc.

PART ONE

Align

CHAPTER ONE

Aligning With the Inner Nudge of our Purpose... and All That Goes With It

MARCIA BENCH

2008 started out like any other year. I was successfully enrolling students from around the world into my career coach training school, speaking on career coaching at various events, and in the midst of updating the 400-page textbook we use to train our students.

But something was beginning to change.

Just doing the same things, day after day and month after month, wasn't working as well. Enrollments were beginning to slip – ever so slightly. And even more importantly, as it became evident that the business was peaking out at its multiple six-figure income level, I was losing my passion about it.

I had already been through a number of significant transitions, both professionally and personally. Before this, the biggest was my move from practicing law to speaking, consulting, and writing books about career transition, business building, and personal transition. And then later, finishing coaching school and starting my coach training institute in the midst of the dot-com bust in 2001 (just 45 days after the idea was given to me to create a school in this new niche), including facing and defeating cancer the following year.

Externally, I was a success. I could live where I wanted to, travel with my business (and indeed spent a full year working from an RV twice and from a yacht one year), but without the purpose and passion behind the work I was doing – and the financial results to validate that I was on track – I was losing my motivation.

Let's face it, when you graduate from school and transition into your first (or next) job, the process is straightforward. You apply, you interview, you are offered the job, and you begin.

As entrepreneurs, the process of transitioning from one area to another (which we will all do – we are creative by nature!) is quite different. It is more gradual. It begins with an inner nudge from our spirit – so quiet that in the beginning we may not even hear it. But if we pay attention (as I began to do), we realize that we are feeling less content, are just a bit more irritable around our family, and don't look forward to our work day as we once did. And if we don't heed this still, small voice and act on it, depression can set in – and it definitely "visited" me periodically during this period of time!

So, here I was, a substantial contributor to our household (since my husband is retired), feeling less contented with what had been my passionate creation seven years ago... and wondering what to do about it. (This was truly the "seven-year itch" of the business owner, just as people experience in relationships!) How could I keep the income flowing in while I explored the cause behind my lagging passion, and tap into what was coming next?

I began by simply listening within, journaling each morning – not to just express my feelings, but to ask a question – and then listening to (and writing down) what my spirit said in response. I began to tap into my invisible guides and higher self more deeply.

I was led to a new mentor through a transformational workshop, and working with him in turn led me to meeting other teachers and mentors – as well as the like-minded colleagues in their networks. I did deep personal work with energy-centered bodyworkers, got intuitive readings, and attended more seminars. And slowly a new idea began to take shape in my mind. I had spent the past two decades (since 1986), first helping people tap into their purpose in their work, and later teaching people how to coach others to do this as well.

As the big shift – economically and spiritually – began to be felt, it became apparent that my next venture was to become a leader, guide, and mentor to those who have a passion for expressing their purpose through their own business (i.e., entrepreneurs).

And so the Institute for Purposeful Entrepreneurship (IPE) was born in November 2008. I began putting the majority of my energy into that company and much less into my established training one. This turned out to be a dangerous move, as a financial blockage led to accumulating debt, and the enrollments in my training programs dropped off sharply in 2009.

As you can understand, I only became more frustrated by this. After all, I was following my calling. Why wasn't the universe providing me with the financial supply I wanted?

Well, it WAS... but more and more of it was coming through IPE, and the natural decline of the training company was occurring. I decided it would be a good time to sell, and offered the company to six different buyers over a twelve-month period. The last and best contender withdrew his offer when he saw the decline in enrollments. It seems he just didn't understand that it was due to the withdrawal of my energy from it – and that the company was still completely viable!

It was tough to let go of the company I had owned for nine years, but I know that one of the principles of life and business is that surrendering to the process – and letting go of what no longer serves us – is essential to growth. I intuitively felt that the training company would have a role in my future, but that it needed to shift to the background for now so that I could pursue IPE with 100 percent alignment and focus.

So, at the end of 2009, I merged the training company into IPE. And amazingly, my income between the two companies for 2009 totaled $50,000 more than the training company had earned on its own the prior year. I WAS being provided for!

I would like to say that from there on it was smooth sailing, that there were never any challenges, and that all was well, but it wouldn't be the entrepreneurial path then, would it? This is truly a much more rigorous learning and growth platform than I ever realized I was signing up for when I began 24 years ago, but I wouldn't trade it for the world either.

With each stage of the unfolding of the business, each new program launch (whether results are staggering or slow), each new book idea, each new client, I am called to a new level of surrender. I am even asked to let go of what people will think if I spend a weekend with a shaman (which I did), learn how to read the Akashic Records (which I do), and do energy work before a coaching call or teleclass. Indeed, my "tribe" of clients and followers want me to do those things. They crave that spiritual connection! When I stepped out and offered a ceremony instead of a goal-setting class at the beginning of the year, we had record attendance! When I ventured into spiritual topics, which feel more aligned with my path, people loved it!

My spirit has blessed me with a big vision for the coming years, and I can't wait to see what else unfolds! And paradoxically, I was even led to bring the training company back to life – with its own online presence – this fall, but now I understand its role in the bigger picture.

Here are some of the lessons I learned to help you on your journey:

1. We are each always provided for. If we appear to have a financial lack, it is simply blocked energy, fear, our own withholding somewhere in our life, something new ready to unfold, or lack of passion. The solution is often an emotional or energetic one – which may mean recommitting to your own purpose in a deeper way.

2. What others think of us is none of our business. We each have our own unique path which I believe was set in motion even before we took birth. Let's honor each other's path and give each other space to be who we truly are, without ridicule or judgment.

3. Following the spiritual and energetic laws and aligning ourselves with them is as essential to growing our businesses as learning marketing, the internet, and finance. Running our business counter to them is like jumping off a building and hoping gravity won't apply this time. The consequences can be devastating!

4. When a new idea is emerging, seeking inner guidance (and perhaps the ear of a mentor or coach, too) will help us determine where to focus our energy – on the old or on the new. Usually it is a bit of both, and the sooner we can graciously and lovingly let go of the old, with integrity, the sooner the universe can fill the energy field of the new idea/venture/book/class.

Surrender to the higher order that wants to unfold through you – and through which you will learn your most important lessons.

MARCIA BENCH is the Purposeful Business Guide and Mentor. An entrepreneur for more than 24 years, Marcia is now one of the world's leading authorities on entrepreneurship, internet service delivery, information product delivery, and incorporating purpose into one's work and business. She is a former attorney and has authored 23 books on entrepreneurship, personal growth, business, and marketing. For Marcia's FREE information kit on Purposeful Entrepreneurship, visit http://tinyurl.com/bizresources.

CHAPTER TWO

Take a Moment and Step Into Your Happiness Gap

CARRIE STRATHMAN BALLARD

Imagine… a new way of thinking, feeling, and acting… a whole new way of being. Living your life on your own terms. Taking the steps of living out the life of your dreams right now.

Does this describe where you are right now? Perhaps you are preparing to step into your next life chapter, but you feel afraid, unsure of how to make it happen. You have doubts and fears that it won't come true. You so want more freedom; better, deeper, more loving relationships; more income; a healthier body; more knowledge; deeper faith; a career that inspires your passion. You want these, but are afraid that when you take that leap of faith, you'll fall into the abyss rather than step into your bliss!

Are you really afraid or do you just not have a clearly defined vision of your passion and true purpose? You know it's there; you've felt it; you've glimpsed it in your mind's eye for a fleeting moment, but just can't quite describe it exactly. Let's take a moment to suspend fear and disbelief and catch a glimpse of your passion and purpose again.

Imagine living your life as you know you are meant to live it. You've been there before. Remember that perfect day, when all was in alignment.

Remembering that day, where were you; what were you doing; how did you feel? Most important, who were you being? Now suspend disbelief and imagine feeling that way again. Get a vision of it in your mind in deep, vibrant detail. Feel the feelings, the thoughts, the actions you were taking. You remember now, don't you? Yeah, that's it. That's the place.

Now imagine this place existing always in your mind. You can access it anytime, any place you choose to. It only takes a moment. You have the time. Make the time daily, many times a day, to do this. You know the saying by Gandhi, "Be the change you wish to see in the world." You are the change – you just need to choose it and choose it often. Others are wanting this change too. There is already a major shift happening in the world – we just need to wake up to it. We need to learn how to take control of making the changes we want to see rather than just responding to circumstances around us and then asking, "Why isn't my life the way I dreamt it should be?

Do you feel you live a double life? Is there a disappointing gap between the image you see in your mind and feel in your heart, and the image you see and feel in the outside world? Hmm… what if you could close the gap between the two? You can, you know. It all begins with you. You are the common denominator here, you see. It's time to take control of your thoughts, feelings, and actions, and bring them into alignment with your vision. Does that feel scary? Don't know how? I bet you do. You just need to believe strongly enough and want it badly enough.

"And the day came when the discomfort to stay tightly in a bud became more than the pain to change."

~ ANAÏS NIN

Just take a moment and see yourself physically creating your world on the outside to be a mirror image of your world on the inside. Cool, huh? Now take this a step further and imagine yourself doing this on a daily basis.

Hmm. "How do I do this and sustain it?" you ask. Great question.

What if every morning your first thoughts were of what you intend to create for that day? What if these small daily actions taken over the period of a week, a month, or 6 months, could snowball into creating a new reality? What if these daily actions created a healthier body and stronger, deeper relationships with yourself and between yourself and others? What if these actions created a career or vocation you are passionate about and you elegantly had more energy and more income?

"Be the change you wish to see in the world."

~ GANDHI

Adopt a daily practice of creating your living environment, a living culture if you will, where everything is supportive of your creating and living your purpose.

Do you have a Daily Success Formula?

1. Remember your purpose and how it will impact the world.
2. Create a compelling vision for how to carry out your purpose.
3. Find the knowledge from experts already doing what you want to do.
4. Apply these actions and knowledge.
5. Create the environment to keep you focused and disciplined to continue taking action daily. This is crucial. Remember that everything in this environment counts!
6. Share your success and knowledge with others for we are here to serve others.
7. Be grateful for what is.

Do you start off each day with a ritual to step into your GAP? I do! When I wake up I start by asking myself what/who am I most GRATEFUL for followed by a 15-30 minute meditation, and then end it with a visualization session of ABUNDANCE I am creating and achieving in each area of my life. I soften and open my heart, then I visualize the endless POSSIBIL-ITY I want to be an example of – just like a photograph or a scene from a motion picture I am writing, directing, and starring in. At times, I add affirmations. I include with this a daily practice of stretches and yoga to wake up and get moving. I eat food that is raw, organic, and alkaline as often as possible.

"Happiness cannot come from without. It must come from within. It is not what we see and touch or that which others do for us which makes us happy; it is that which we think and feel and do, first for the other fellow and then for ourselves."

~ HELEN KELLER

Step into how this new world you are creating feels. Now imagine this for the rest of your life. Or not. Which feels better? Which feels right? If it feels uncomfortable, then good! It is right. It is the next step for you to take, isn't it? Remember, if you are not growing, then you are dying. You know in your heart that is true. Which do you choose for yourself and for those you love?

Create this life you've just imagined with other like-minded individuals who yearn for this growth and personal evolution just as you do. Imagine being supported to take this vision you've created in your mind's eye. Imagine it is a photograph. Now what if you could find a group of people who would support you in resizing your photograph to life-size? It would be amazing, wouldn't it?

CARRIE STRATHMAN BALLARD is the CEO and Founder of GIVE, the Global Institute of Visionary Executives, an innovative association for creators and big thinkers ready to step into their next life chapter. Learn to suspend disbelief, connect to spirit, and step elegantly into your best life now! To download your FREE meditation, "Build your personal roadmap into your next life chapter," and learn more about the transformation waiting for you, please visit www.GIVE-connect.com.

CHAPTER THREE

Higher State of Consciousness

BILL BAREN

I have been blessed to study under many amazing mentors since I began my personal development journey. One of these mentors stands out head and shoulders above the rest. It is through paying attention to this teacher that I have created all of my success. It is through personal immersion in the lessons so expertly laid out for me by my teacher that I have been able to deepen my understanding of who I am, of the natural laws of the universe, and of the people on this planet. Through the relationship with my teacher I have been forever changed.

At this point, you're probably wondering who this wise sage might be. It's…

MY BUSINESS.

Yes, my business is my swami, my guru, my spiritual teacher. My business never fails to let me know when I am out of alignment. My business always rewards me when I am on the right path. It always nudges me in the direction of being more conscious in my interactions with my team, with my clients, and with everyone who comes into contact with me through my outreach efforts. The more I am being authentically me, the more my audience responds, and the greater the impact of my work, the more financial success I attract.

In this chapter, I want to share with you three of my most impactful lessons that have allowed me to create conscious success in my life.

LESSON #1: HOW YOUR BUSINESS IS LIKE A HOT AIR BALLOON

Ever since I was a kid and I saw the movie Around the World in 80 Days, I have been fascinated with hot air ballooning. In the movie, I was mesmerized by the serenity and beauty of these amazing inflatable flying balls.

To this day, I find the mechanics of how to travel great distances in a balloon intriguing. You see, it's not always easy to get to your destination via this method. Just because you want to go east doesn't necessarily mean the wind always cooperates. What if the wind is blowing west when you want to go east?

No amount of fighting against the wind gets you to your destination. Fighting against the forces of nature is truly a fruitless venture.

So, what do you do when the wind is not co-operating?

What experienced balloonists do is to simply increase their altitude until the winds are blowing in the perfect direction to get them to where they want to go. One of the ways to increase altitude is by dropping unnecessary weight out of the balloon. Also, because balloons move with the wind, when you are at the optimal altitude, you feel absolutely no wind – there is no resistance.

I have always found my business to operate very much like a balloon. My business has taught me never to fight against the natural flow of the universe. When I am not getting to my destination (my goals) in my business, I can't fight against the winds to get there. It's pointless.

It is precisely during the periods in my business when the going is not easy – when clients aren't signing up, when sales are down, when it's hard to inspire my team, when I am frustrated, and when I am feeling overwhelmed by the sheer weight of everything I have to do – it is during those moments I've learned to remember to change my altitude.

Working harder, longer hours and just putting in more effort is the equivalent of fighting against the wind. When I find myself going into this lifelong pattern of pushing and trying too hard, my business reminds me that cultivating my capacity to lift myself to a higher state of development and a higher state of consciousness is the real key to my success. It's what allows my business to effortlessly flow to my destination. When I shed the weight of the conditioning, societal expectations and familiar patterning, I begin to elevate, and when I do, nothing gets in my way. I don't feel the wind of resistance.

Then and only then can I produce the impact I want to create. It is only then that I attract unprecedented abundance into my life. It is only then that I feel like the universe is literally conspiring to give me exactly what I want.

It is only then that I feel like I am flow.

LESSON #2: NOTHING WORKS UNLESS I WORK IT

I had read hundreds of business books. I had studied many systems and philosophies of business success. I had followed the teachings of many business experts.

Yet nothing seemed to work for me. I was still struggling. I was still barely getting by. I was still working a lot and getting very little in return.

I kept thinking, "What's wrong with me? Why is it that despite how much I want my coaching business to succeed, I am failing? Why do all of these seemingly great teachings fail ME?"

It was during a period of depressed questioning five years ago; it was out of the rubble of a business that was not working; it was during that state that I finally got the second most significant lesson in my business: Nothing works unless I work it.

That's right! Every piece of advice has the potential to be good if I truly apply it and make it my own. All of the teachings are brilliant in their own way only if I connect them to my own brilliance. Information is not enough. I actually have to apply and adjust the information to my own business. I have to IMPLEMENT what I am learning.

Once I had that epiphany, everything started to click. It is through my action that all of the teachings I have ever studied miraculously came together to create an amazing tapestry of success.

Only if I dedicate myself to truly understanding the spirit behind the teaching; only if I commit to applying what I am learning fully; only if I adopt the lesson to my life, to my business, to my personality, do the teachings actually come alive.

Nothing anyone ever teaches me is gospel. It is simply an opportunity for me to experiment, get into action, and see how I can produce my desired results.

Turns out:

EVERYTHING WORKS.

But here's the kicker. Everything works only if I work it.

When I hear clients complain that somebody's teaching, blueprint, or system has not produced results for them, I ask, "How much of the teaching have you actually implemented? How have you personalized the formula to your situation? How committed were you to getting the results you wanted?"

I remind them that everything works when you operate in a higher state of consciousness. Everything works when you work it.

LESSON #3: IT'S NOT ABOUT ME

The last big shift in my business that I want to share with you is the realization that my business is not about me.

I know it's seems counter-intuitive. How can my business, which is built around me, be not about me? Then who is my business really about?

My business is about my tribe. It's about the people I am meant to serve. It is really about being guided to tapping into the greatest need of my audience and about producing the results they want most.

How did this shift manifest in my business?

The focus of my marketing changed. I stopped selling me. I started giving my clients what they want. And what they want is results.

Nobody wants to buy me. Just that thought alone is liberating.

I no longer talk to people about what I do and see their eyes glaze over. I am no longer in the business of coaching. I am now in the business of helping business owners who want to make a difference by getting all the clients they want.

Now I know what I am promising. Now I know what I need to focus my efforts on. Now I know what I am committed to. And now my audience knows what they get from working with me.

My business is now truly about YOU and not about me.

This subtle shift has been revolutionary for me. It has helped me quadruple my audience and double my revenue in less than a year. It has allowed me to feel more on purpose then ever in my business. It has liberated me from focusing too much on myself and how others may perceive me.

It has given me freedom.

It is not my intention to make it sound like getting these lessons from my business has been easy. My business is not always the kindest of teachers, but when I do listen, when I stop resisting what is, and when I hear the unadulterated truth from my business – magic happens. I become more authentic. I am guided every step of the way.

And guess what.

My business grows as I grow. It is my teacher's way of telling me I'm on the right track.

BILL BAREN is a top business coach dedicated to helping conscious business owners get new clients and grow their businesses. He is the founder of Bill Baren Coaching and produced many successful live and on-line programs: Client Mastery Blueprint, The Big Shift Experience, Ultimate Entrepreneur Toolkit, and Master of Enrollment. You can get his FREE report, "10 Secrets to Getting New Clients to Say Yes… And Hire You Right On The Spot" at www.BillBaren.com/secrets.

CHAPTER FOUR

Following
a Vision

YVONNE GONZALEZ-BAEZ

One Sunday night, while meditating at my home in Mexico, I had a vision:

I am standing in front of a lake with a huge smile on my face; one that radiates satisfaction, peace and success. I am about ten years older than I am right now, since there are more grey hairs on my head and wrinkles in my face, showing that the path was hard at first but had its rewards. The authentic "me" shines all over. My beauty comes more from within, from the certainty that I have accomplished my life's purpose. An aura of wisdom and peace surrounds me.

About fifty feet behind me is a lovely cottage. A bearded man with hair down to his shoulders walks from the cottage with two mugs of hot tea: one for him and one for me. He stands at my left side, hugs me, and embraces the moment with the same satisfaction and peace. I immediately sense we are happily together. We both have loved and been loved; have kept healthy; raised our children to become happy, assertive beings, and have made a difference in this world by building a conscious business helping many people get an enriching existence.

Intuitively I know all this takes place in Canada!

My life, though, at the time of the vision, was far from being satisfactory and peaceful. My husband and I were almost strangers living under the same roof, struggling with financial issues. I was also in constant fear of something happening to our daughter, realizing how crime was rising in my beloved country, Mexico. I wanted a better life – one that could give us prosperity, peace of mind and a more secured future, especially for my daughter.

By then, I had written a national award-winning book and had my own conscious business of massage oils for the seven chakras, handmade by Down syndrome young adults, but still something didn't feel right. I wasn't aligned with my higher self and was living in fear. But after the vision, something shifted. I knew exactly what I had to do: move to Canada.

I recalled receiving a spam message two months prior from a Canadian immigrant agency inviting me to apply for a Permanent Resident Visa. For who knows what reason, I didn't delete the message, but kept it in one of my folders. Now I understand that my subconscious was already working in what eventually was going to become my spiritual path!

The next morning I turned on the computer and immediately found that spam email. I replied to it, requesting more information about how to apply. By the end of that day I had been contacted by the agency and had started the process of becoming Canadian residents. When I approached my husband and told him the plan, he was supportive, but over time he started getting even more focused on his work and personal career, taking us further apart.

"God's timing is perfect," I kept reminding myself, when months passed and we had no news from the Canadian Embassy. Two years later, when they told us that the final requests were compiled, I started to get unsettled, since our financial circumstances were still rough and the savings to move to Canada were slim. My business was still running, but at a very slow pace, so I asked my spirit guides to help me get a steady income. Out of the blue I was rehired at an international school in the same position I held and loved years earlier! This time, though, the job was very stressful and much more demanding than before. It was very hard to keep up with it and I constantly got sick, but I saw it as a venue for accomplishing my goal and remained strong. "It's only for a year," I kept telling myself, knowing that it was the means to my goal. The timing was making it happen and I only needed to work on the financial matter to let the Universe know that I was serious about my intention! I was committed to save every single penny earned from that job.

I was also blessed because my daughter had gotten a scholarship to study at that school, so we no longer had to pay for her very expensive tuition. All that, indeed, helped us to achieve the monetary goal in exactly one year! My biggest concern was well taken care of, and as a bonus my daughter's English skills were strengthened by studying there!

We finally got the visas as Canadian Permanent Residents in May, 2009. I was ready to fly in July, but the timing to make the move still belonged to the spiritual realm. Prior my departure, my dear brother, who had donated one of his kidneys to me almost 20 years before, got severely sick. I managed to travel to Puerto Vallarta where he lived and was able to be with him during his last days, comforting him with the assurance that he was going to still be alive through me. I was able to say "good-bye" to him and come to terms with the most grateful gift of life he once gave me by being as close to him as possible, and not thousands of miles away, should I have left for Canada before!

I hadn't had time to pack or to sell the things I was going to get rid of. So, after his passing away, and while I was still mourning, I rescheduled my trip. We found out that my husband was required to come with me and my daughter, since he was the main applicant in the visa process. He couldn't get time off to take us during the summer. So we set the departure date for the 10th of September. Therefore, the 9th of the 9th month of 2009 – a very spiritual date – was my last day in my beloved country of origin. I was ready to take the next step towards my vision.

Overall, it took us more than three years to get the visas and make the move, but my hope never ceased. The vision was crystal clear and I knew I was going to be led to it at the perfect time.

Now I am in Calgary, Alberta, where my spirit and intuition took me, and not Toronto, Ontario, where we first thought we would move to. My husband is still in Mexico. I thank him for his support during the whole project, and respect his decisions, but I know my destiny was to come to Canada, with or without him. It was time for me to be in charge of my own life!

The arrival and settlement was a piece of cake, mostly because through meditation I had already envisioned a smooth shift. I met, over the internet, my now beloved landlords who, for a very reasonable rate, leased us a furnished suite with utilities and appliances included, and with no long-term contracts, so we could get to know the city before signing a longer rental commitment. My daughter landed "as a fish in a pond" at a school where peers greeted and welcomed her openly. Now she is also able to ride her bike all over the place, with no fear of being kidnapped!

As for me, I am re-starting my path as a speaker, writer, and meditation and spiritual-wellness coach, to help others transform their life's challenging events into something inspiring. Only seven months after my arrival, I was invited to give public speeches at an immigrant experience conference at the Kidney March Opening Expo, and led a poetry reading in Spanish. I have also volunteered at the Calgary Public Library as a "living book," where I share how I aim to live life at its best, honoring my deceased brother who lives through me as I promised him. I also enjoy helping others express their success and reach their goals before it gets to be too late!

I trust that my spirit guides are supporting me every step of the way. Since I am being true to my nature, my call, the vision I had and my mission to help others, my life is being sorted out and prosperity IS coming my way.

The lake, the cottage, the lovely partner, and the hot tea are waiting for me somewhere in the future… and I'll meet them there, you bet!

So, based on my experience, I recommend that once you decide to follow your own spiritual journey, you:

- Trust your intuition, vision, and/or inner wisdom to be what you know you are meant to be.
- Understand that the time for things to happen will come.
- Focus on your vision; keep meditating.
- Don't let anything or anyone distract you from your intention.
- Take any needed actions in the physical realm, so that when the time comes you are prepared to make the opportunity meet your goals, or in other words: "Get in the spiritual train and move towards your next destination: Success!"

YVONNE GONZALEZ-BAEZ is an award-winner writer from Mexico who moved to Canada aligned with what her spirit was showing her to do. Currently she can help you connect with your inner self to realize what your spirit's call is and work towards a more successful and enriching existence. She provides chakra balancing, meditation and visualization sessions, spiritual coaching, writing workshops, and public speeches. Visit her website www.ExpressYourSuccess.net and begin a spiritual journey towards your own realization!

CHAPTER FIVE

Doctor, the Patient is Waiting!

ROBERT L. BRIDGES, MD

The gathered physicians had assembled in the gallery of the operating theater to watch the complex surgery. The famous surgeon entered the operating suite of the equally famous hospital and moved to the operating table, the patient already unconscious from induction of anesthesia. The surgeon turned to his audience and commenced discussing the surgery. He talked and talked and talked. Finally, the chief resident, in what could have been a career-ending move in those days, picked up a pair of clamps and whacked the famed surgeon over his gloved knuckles. When eyes met eyes, the chief resident only had to say, "Doctor, the patient is waiting!"

Whether your "patient" is conscious or not, they need to know that they are your priority. In any business, one can exchange "client" for "patient." In starting a new business, the client is always waiting; waiting for a newer product, a better replacement for an existing service, or to just have more choices. Your arrival on the scene must evoke the realization that the wait is over and the moment has come to make the move.

Over the past forty years, I have had the opportunity to pioneer businesses in two distinctly separate professions in Alaska. In each, business models were well developed elsewhere, but absent in these locales, requiring an implicit, in-depth professional knowledge of the business to compensate for shortcomings of resources and capital. These endeavors were pioneering commercial radio broadcasting in rural "bush" Alaska in the 1960s and 1970s, and later in 2001, participating in creating the first freestanding multi-center medical imaging group in Alaska. While the latter business did not require hanging power and telephone lines from trees, dodging bears, and facing arctic storms as the former did, both required total commitment and above all an all-consuming passion to see dreams create reality.

Starting in the 1950s, my father engineered and built over 40 radio stations with several being in Alaska. Building our own radio station, the first civilian one on Kodiak Island, was a shoestring endeavor at best. (The Coast Guard base had an Armed Forces Radio Network feed for the base.) These areas did not have local radio service and the stations became a pipeline of news and information to the outlying areas. Classic for these stations were the "bush messages," sending news and personal communications to the listeners where there were no phones or two-way radios. "Trapline Chatter," made famous by KJNP in the Interior of Alaska, would become "Kodiak Crabbers" for our station.

With resources for just about everything so limited on Kodiak Island, I had no choice but to have a hands-on approach. To say I was multi-tasking would be an understatement. When we did not have enough money to clear the land for the antenna site, I wound up buying a 20-inch roller-tipped Stihl chainsaw and cutting down three acres of heavy timber the summer prior to entering graduate school. When the station needed an announcer, graduate school ended, along with any chance to bolster my academic credentials for medical school applications. When the electronics repairman, hired as engineer, failed to adequately maintain the transmitter, I took correspondence courses and boosted my 3rd class to a 1st class FCC license to do the maintenance myself. To help run the station, I designed a computer-based automation system using an Apple II because commercial systems were too expensive. The control room doubled as my bedroom at night as I signed off and then on again the next morning. The first night on Kodiak would have been tough had I not literally found money on the street to buy dinner.

Despite these hardships, what sustained my passion for running the radio station? A profound relationship developed between the listeners and the station, be it the announcement of a Coast Guard commendation for helping to save a ship at sea, or letting a bush family know that all was well with a hospitalized relative or a new birth. Such events provided palpable joy and satisfaction in helping others.

The lessons of tenacity and perseverance served me well as I undertook my second career – medicine. Instead of wearing all of the hats, I came to realize and truly understand the importance of specialization and delegation of responsibilities.

In the early 1990s, I hit a time of the doldrums. My medical practice was running smoothly, albeit a little dry and boring. Then the paradigm changed. Combined with the early stages of the internet era, a unified medical industry standard to send images to and from other scanners at medical centers and hospitals was introduced. Here was a new set of challenges and opportunities. I could now draw from my communications background to expand our group's networking capability. This time the "listeners" were the physicians. For timely consultation, not only could we disseminate the important imaging data directly to the doctors at their offices, to the operating room, or late at night to their homes, but also to the whole world of specialists. Sharing critical information shortened the time from medical imaging to actual patient care. I found that I could take experience drawn from a totally different field and apply it to this new one.

Over the years, on our "red-eye" flights to and from Alaska, my wife and I saw plane-loads of people – in casts, on crutches or clutching ice bags to their jaws after having had surgery – who had gone "outside" Alaska for medical care. There were definitely big challenges regarding how to improve medical care within the state. Opportunity arose to create a "hybrid" medical group – a medical imaging center with a small staff on the ground in Alaska combined with my group's larger practice in California. Linked via a secure internet network, a practice was created that had the economy of a smaller start-up while also having the functional capabilities of a larger specialized group of physicians.

In 2001, a core group of owners dedicated to serving Alaskans was assembled. Launching the imaging center required the majority to pool their life savings to swing the purchase of the first MRI scanner. These were medical imaging technologists who had worked for years for doctors and hospitals, who now saw a need for an imaging center to add a viable choice to the limited services available in Alaska. We set out to break the glass ceiling of exclusivity usually reserved for doctors only. Having been on the ground floor of building five imaging centers in California in the 1990s, I didn't have to bring a chainsaw this time, but I did bring up a telemedicine computer system I had created for my California medical group. True to form, I did wind up sleeping at the center for the first months in part to cover night-time calls for hospitals back in California using the teleradiology system I created. From this original center, there is now a state-wide network of four.

What has helped me sustain the passion? In great part, I am daily selling the best product I have to offer… myself. Whether playing the next record, reading the next news item, or diagnosing a problem with modern medical equipment, my personal input is the final true "value added" to the product. What I am after is a return customer or a new referral. The reward is the request for consultation from physicians seeking my input and recommendations, and ultimately helping the patient get the best diagnosis possible to speed their healing.

I have found that I can take the experiences of different business models and adapt them to the new business. As an example, I got an early jump on telemedicine from my days in commercial broadcasting. I have found that breakthroughs can come from outside of a standard business model.

Passion also has been sustained by successfully taking on new challenges. I recognize that the greatest reward may not come from outside recognition, but from the personal satisfaction from a job well done. Most people will never know, nor probably appreciate, the hard work and long hours put into the business to make it a success. It is the fortunate entrepreneur who has a family that shares the same passion and willingness to bear the same sacrifices to make the business succeed. My passion is sustained because of my wife's passion for our life's endeavors.

Finally, I have come to an understanding that life and businesses are, for the long term, like a marathon, not a sprint. I leave you with these lines that have guided me through some very tough times.

"Let us throw off everything that hinders... and let us run with perseverance the race marked out for us.... so that you will not grow weary and lose heart."

~ HEBREWS 12:1-3 NIV

After all, "The patient is waiting..."

ROBERT L. BRIDGES, MD, is a double-boarded physician (radiology and nuclear medicine) and former assistant professor (UC-Irvine) who has been in private practice since 1987. Broadcasting experience, including early pioneer-radio days in Alaska, contributed greatly to the success of Alaska Open Imaging Center, of which he is part-owner and medical director. Holder of medical patents, well-published in medical journals, and requested lecturer on advanced medical imaging, Dr. Bridges was a team consultant in launching nine imaging centers. For information visit www.RobertLBridgesMD.com.

CHAPTER SIX

What Happened to Your Real Life?

ANITA CRAWFORD CLARK

The doctor had pulled us aside just moments before and given us the grim news: "After running extensive tests, we have concluded that there is no brain activity. There is nothing more we can do for him. His body is shutting down fast," she said, in that cold way in which doctors seem to communicate. "But we want you to consider donating his organs. There isn't much time, so you need to make a decision now, otherwise the window for donating his organs will close."

She left the room, leaving the four of us there to make one of the most heart-wrenching decisions I pray no family should ever have to make. We hugged, we cried, we discussed it, and we decided that if we could spare another family from the ache of losing such a loved one, then we would donate his organs. Waiting for us and waiting to hear the doctor's diagnosis, was a room full of relatives and friends. The tears in my father's eyes were enough to send a message to everyone that we would be saying our final farewell.

We walked through the throng of family and friends, which filled the ICU, so much so that I was surprised they let everyone in at the same time. The four of us made our way to Rawland's room and that's where I found myself holding his hand and asking just one more time, "God… Lord, please perform a miracle right now." I squeezed his hand tightly as if that would somehow stimulate his brain. As I stood there holding my brother's hand, gazing upon him for the last time, trying to be strong for my father and two sisters, somehow I felt I had let my brother down. I felt that same sense of helplessness I had felt six years earlier when my mother lost her battle against lung cancer. All I could do was stare at the beautiful life that was about to leave this world forever.

Many significant shifts surfaced in my life not long after I lost my brother. I shifted from hoping I would realize my dreams, to outright dogged determination to achieve them. I embarked on a quest of expecting and manifesting miraculous outcomes. Why miraculous? Life – every day, minute, second – whatever the smallest measurement of time is – now meant more to me than ever before. I now recognized every breath as miraculous. I took nothing for granted. My dreams from then on were non-negotiable.

I was no longer willing to trade in, sacrifice, or delay my dreams. Up until then I had not been living my real life. I was living the life I thought would please everyone else and directed eighty-five percent of my time and effort to that end. I tried to use the other fifteen percent to follow my dreams, my passions. I did not realize that I needed to switch those percentages around. I was under bondage to the task master of "please everyone else first." I served it and so did my brother.

I desired to be free. I wanted freedom from doing what others expected of me. I wanted freedom from that look of approval from parents, pastors, family, friends, and colleagues. Why did I need that so much? Why couldn't I break free? What was the worst that could have happened had I gone out and lived my real life? Most entrepreneurs hear all too often those negative, dream-killing, stay-in-bondage messages from well-meaning family and friends. We hear it from our government. We hear it from the media. We hear it from college professors. So, how do most people break free? Most don't!

Most people say they want freedom – whether that's financial freedom or freedom to be their own boss, to accomplish some grand goal, or to realize a lifelong dream. But they have become accustomed to their task master and lifestyle, and they do not realize it until the first real test of courage, perseverance, and faith is staring them in the face.

Most people are like the children of Israel. They also wanted to be free. In fact, they prayed for four hundred years for their freedom. Finally, the day of freedom came. There they were, camped out in front of the Red Sea. They were free. They're prayers had been answered. They had a promise. They had a leader. They had God!

Moses had led them out of Egypt. All was well… until they saw Pharaoh's chariots charging towards them in the distance. Fear set in. The first thing they started doing was blaming Moses for getting them into that mess, even though they had prayed for freedom. They wanted freedom – so long as it was easy. The moment they hit their first challenge they were ready to crawl back to a life of bondage. I can only imagine the things they shouted at Moses. "We would have been better off staying in Egypt. Yeah, at least we had food and shelter. We had it pretty good back in Egypt."

For most people, at the first challenge they meet, they start in on themselves with self-doubt. They second-guess their decision to step out and live their dream. They wonder if they would have been better off staying where they were. But thank God Moses did not give in to their fears, doubts, and accusations. His modern day response might have been, "Are you kidding me? You were slaves. Have you forgotten about the beatings and working yourselves into an early grave to make someone else rich? Have you forgotten how that madman murdered your first born baby boys? That's what you are whining about?"

Most people would rather be a slave to a life without purpose than face the challenge of breaking free. They would exchange their freedom for a false sense of security. They would rather live the life that happens to them, instead of going for the most amazing life they can get, period.

The children of Israel were willing to go back to a life of bondage, of false security. But Moses had a purpose, a goal, a dream from which he was not willing to back down even when staring at a seemingly insurmountable obstacle – the Red Sea.

Even with no possible way of escape. No means to cross the sea. No boats. No rafts. Nothing!

He was true to his purpose.

Even as the enemy was approaching and imminent death was upon him and all those who had followed him. No weapons to turn and fight. No swords. No shields. Nothing!

He honored his goal.

Even though everyone around him was shouting and screaming at him, "Turn back! Give up! Quit! You can't succeed! It was a dumb idea! There's no hope! Make a deal with Pharaoh! Get your old job back! Take the money! You're not smart enough!"

He held fast to his dream.

You have to have that kind of determination. You have to make that kind of commitment to your goals, dreams, and purpose. When you are up against your Red Sea, and all these challenges are charging your way, testing your faith, your beliefs, your perseverance, and there seems to be no way of retreat or escape… that is when you will know you are living and/ or on course to living your real life.

If you will stand your ground, if you will trust, believe, and hold fast to your dream, you will see the waters between you and your real life start to part. You will walk on dry land and cross over to your dreams, and all the problems, naysayers, and challenges will be drowned by the waters of perseverance. When you cross over, your problems can not follow you. It is the person you have become that will be of greatest value to you.

My brother's stroke at age forty-four and his untimely death knocked the wind out of me. Breathing was difficult. I had to re-discover the meaning and purpose in life – my life. Why am I here? What is it I'm supposed to be doing? What excites me? What inspires me? What am I passionate about? And am I filling my time doing these things? Are you?

It took me a year to truly understand my purpose in life. I decided to dust off one of my children's book manuscripts and start submitting it again. It was accepted on my first attempt and will be published in 2011. I decided to use my gift for teaching and speaking, so now I'm an inspirational speaker and social media consultant. I have a chapter in this book – how cool is that? I have met some of the most remarkable people on the planet. It just sort of started unfolding once I declared and accepted that I owed it to myself to live my real life, to honor my dreams. I discovered my purpose, backed it with passion and I am living it with joy.

We all have an awesome responsibility – that is to HONOR OUR DREAMS!

As a former Christian school teacher and vice principal, *ANITA CRAWFORD CLARK* developed the natural ability to take complex information and simplify it, which has made her a popular speaker and trainer. To learn more about this mother of three, inspirational speaker, children's book writer, and social media consultant, and to obtain your FREE MP3 download of the first three chapters of her ebook: *Inspired GOALS: Growing Over All Limitations Spiritually*, visit www.AnitaCrawfordClark.com.

CHAPTER SEVEN

"Being" in Business: Using Your Gift of Intuition in Business

MARY DENARO

Back in 1982, two partners and I decided to start a Center for Intuitive Development as soon as we had a building. We were eager to answer the call of our students. They wanted to go further into their studies of energy awareness, meditation, self-healing and reading energy.

Six months later we still had no building. The agent had told us that the real estate market was tight, with very few rentals available. So, we waited for a building. And we waited. And we waited some more.

Then intuitive messages started coming up during my morning meditation, telling me that we needed to start our center without a building. These messages kept coming, although they did not feel logical to my partners or to me. However, we were teaching intuition to others, so we knew we needed to honor our own intuitive guidance. So, we made the decision to start our center without a building and called our students to tell them the news.

Three days later, the real estate agent called us. A building had just been put on the rental market which was exactly what we wanted with workshop spaces, small rooms for energy readings and healings, and an office. It was ideal!

This experience reaffirmed the power of my intuitive wisdom. It always speaks the truth!

For over three decades, I have had the opportunity to help thousands of people awaken to their soul's purpose and embody their intuition. It's been a delight to mentor hundreds of successful entrepreneurs and executives, and help them discover their inner success.

Then in 2008, my intuition spoke to me through a crystal-clear vision during meditation; I saw my hand turning the page of a book, closing a chapter, and beginning a new chapter filled with golden light. It was now time to surrender to a challenging time in my life. I was being urged to let go.

I wondered about the bright golden light on the new page in the book of my life which would soon begin. Three days later, I experienced a clear inner knowing that I was being called to contribute in a much larger way to the evolution of consciousness now taking place. I wondered how I would do this. Even though I am not very tech savvy, I was drawn to my computer and discovered a new world. I learned that teleseminars were being used to reach people on a global level. This was the answer! I could start to reach hundreds, perhaps thousands of people worldwide by giving teleseminars and creating an internet-based business!

That summer of 2008, when I started to learn about internet marketing, I was full of passion, inspiration and motivation … I wanted to learn it all! In October and November, I flew from the Netherlands to do workshops in Atlanta and Los Angeles.

For me, "being" in business, has always felt like an inside job. It's about being who I am deep in my heart, and from this state of being comes a movement or impulse from within my soul, to blend this state of being with action or "doing." From this energy vibration of being, the experience of doing happens with ease, pleasure and joy.

Yet gradually, over the months, I began losing my joy and excitement. I was starting from a place of "doing" instead of "being." An old pattern of perfectionism had surfaced.

I became overly-driven… doing, doing, and more doing! By November, 2008, I would stay up half the night doing teleseminars at least three times each week. Many of them began at 2:00 a.m. Dutch time. After a few hours of sleep, I began yet another full day of work. I did this for 6 months.

I was off my path… out of alignment. My "retired perfectionist" and "pusher" were now more or less running the show. Driven by both, I set unrealistic deadlines for starting my online business. I had allowed my analytical mind to become dominant. There was now much too much chatter to hear the gentle voice of my intuition!

I was no longer "walking my talk." I no longer took time for my daily yoga, meditation, and body-breath work. I was leading a double life of learning all night, followed by a full day of work by day.

Then in May, 2009, my whole life suddenly changed. While driving, I saw two white cars coming towards me. I closed one eye … and saw only one white car. Something was terribly wrong with my eyesight.

After extensive medical tests, the neurologist's opinion was that a small blood clot had caused double vision and, later, problems with my concentration. When I meditated, I found that the familiar "landscape" of my left brain had changed completely.

This was a gigantic wake-up call. The deadlines for my internet business became insignificant. I cancelled all the trainings I was scheduled to give or assigned them to others. Suddenly, nothing was more important than my health and healing.

It was time to surrender on every level. It was time to clear out old clutter – spiritually, physically and emotionally – from my office, my home and my body. It was time to ask for help and let go of the old belief that I needed to do everything myself. It was time to delegate and outsource. My new motto was, "Every day is take care of Mary day."

Yet something very deep inside resisted complete surrender to my present situation.

Deep in meditation, my intuition revealed the source: my belief from my teens that to totally surrender meant to accept an outmoded, old-world belief that limited women. For me then, that meant collapse, and allowing my spirit to shrivel and die! My revelation now was that surrendering meant listening to what my soul needed, to accept help in my life and in my business.

Once I released the belief, my body tingled. Instead of collapsing and shriveling, I felt expansion and exhilaration. I felt intense love, gratitude and joy, and something very, very new... an experience of spiritual bliss!

As I let go of needing to do everything by myself, I experienced a deeper spiritual experience of surrendering to my source, to God, to the universe, and a new sense of peace and freedom. I felt aligned with my true self and in the flow!

The intuitive wisdom and knowledge that couldn't reach me because I had been too busy "doing," now flooded into my life. As I took more time for my spiritual practice and writing, I received a treasure chest of gifts that deepened my spiritual path and my soul-based business.

Back to "being"... and "being" in business.

Today, the page has turned in my book of life to the bright, sparkling, golden light! I am healthy and healed. I feel aligned, in sync, with an enormous feeling of expansion. The transformational journey has enriched my experience of being of service. Amazing opportunities are flowing to me in my life and business. My online business, which had been put on the back burner, has been moved forward. And there's some great cooking going on!

Your soul speaks to you through your intuition. I am listening again! I learned that it's easy to get too busy to hear the voice of your own intuition.

When you embrace your intuition, you can do so with trust, knowing that intuition usually defies logic. That's how it works.

Becoming a conscious entrepreneur and using your intuition to guide you is an exciting, rich, and empowering experience, full of joy and wonder. I invite you to begin with these 7 steps:

1. Say yes to it! Feel the yes in your heart. (This creates conscious awareness.)
2. Come into a state of being. Use Buddha Belly Breathing to help you quiet your analytical mind and become fully present in the moment.
3. Ask a simple question for which the answer is yes or no.
4. Allow the answer to come to you.
5. Appreciate and thank your intuition!
6. Act immediately from inspiration on the message you receive.
7. Witness the outcome… and celebrate!

Here's how to practice Buddha Belly Breathing (breathe in, belly goes out):

*   Put your hand on your belly.
*   Allow your attention to drop down into your belly. Feel your hand (palm) on your belly from inside.
*   As you inhale, allow your belly to expand until you have a Buddha belly.
*   As you exhale, allow your navel to move back towards your spine, and feel your Buddha belly disappear.
*   Do this for a few minutes while you enjoy your Buddha belly.

As you act on your intuition, its messages will become clearer and stronger. It has always been there waiting for you; now is the time to align with it. When you do, you will experience, as I have, that your intuition is a gift from your soul for you and your soul-based business, a gift of wisdom, comfort, and crystal-clear guidance.

MARY DENARO is a pioneer in intuitive development and healing, co-founder of the first Center for Intuitive Development in Western Europe in 1982. As mentor, trainer, and spiritual teacher, she is passionate about helping heart-based entrepreneurs embody their gift of intuition so they experience crystal-clear clarity in making decisions, more ease and vitality, and create a life and business in sync: success from the inside out! Get your FREE ebook *Becoming Your Own Intuitive* at www.BecomingYourOwnIntuitive.com.

CHAPTER EIGHT

The Washing of the Feet: Step into Your Unique Path of Service

LUZ LILIANA GARCIA, PH.D.

The soft glow from the skylights accentuated the surreal feeling of this night. The chapel was completely full; every seat was taken by children, students, adults, and clergy. Some wore their Sunday best, while most of the students wore their blue jeans and T-shirts. To an observer, this may have seemed a regular Sunday church day, but this was no ordinary church day for me. To start with, it was not even Sunday, and I was not sitting in my usual place in the rear corner of the chapel. Instead, this was Thursday night, and I was sitting with eleven other people at the altar in front of the congregation.

As the service began, I thought, "I don't deserve to be here. Why did they choose me? It doesn't make any sense. I hardly know anyone here. I have just been coming to mass everyday for the past few months, and I don't even come on Sundays. I avoid the crowds that come for the usual 'day of obligation.' I enjoy the quiet services with the dozen or fewer people who come regularly on weekdays. I still don't know why they chose me. All I recall is that one time the church secretary asked me after mass to help stuff some envelopes. On this special day, I feel so honored, but I don't think I deserve it."

"The Gospel according to John…" As the lecturer spoke these words, I was brought back from my introspections. The re-enactment of the Washing of the Feet had begun. I observed how the other eleven men and women sitting at the altar with me began removing their shoes and socks, prompting me to do the same.

The priest removed his majestic purple robe, carefully folded it, and handed it to one of the acolytes. Wearing his white tunic and a white cord around his waist, the priest adjusted a pristine hand towel. The acolytes assisted him by carrying a basin and a white, enameled pitcher filled with warm water. The priest knelt in front of the twelve people that had been chosen, re-creating an ancient ceremony that 2,000 years earlier Jesus had performed with his disciples.

As I watched the priest wash the feet of the first person, I imagined the scene 2,000 years earlier. In my mind's eye, the disciples wore tunics very similar to that of Father John, and had traveled down hot, sandy, dusty roads in open-toed sandals. Yes, their feet were dirty, callused, and blistered. I envisioned Jesus, their teacher and master, whom they served out of respect, kneeling by their dusty feet and washing them. They may have felt the same way as I was feeling: undeserving!

I sensed the priest washing the feet of the person next to me. I refocused once again on my surroundings. As the priest knelt in front of me, I noticed his white complexion matched the white hairs that were showing in his otherwise blond, curly hair. He gently looked at me with his blue eyes, and his strong hands tenderly guided my feet into the basin one after the other. Two of the acolytes were kneeling on each side of Father John, each with a separate task. One carried the pitcher full of warm water while the other held fresh towels. The priest slowly poured the water onto my feet. I gazed at them inside the basin; soap bubbles fizzled in the water around them, releasing a delicate fragrance from the water.

The water surrounding my feet felt like a soft embrace by invisible hands, blossoming into a wondrous feeling throughout my entire body, concentrated in my heart. As I basked in these feelings, Father John took my feet out of the basin and softly dried them, and suddenly, to my amazement, he kissed one of them. I cycled through a mixture of emotions. I felt joy. I felt guilt. I felt honored. I felt unworthy. Even after I felt these feelings, I was unprepared for what came next.

The priest, in his role as Jesus, lifted his head and with his soft blue eyes, looked deeply into mine and, sternly and slowly, spoke the following words: **"Come follow me! Be my disciple**!" I was completely overwhelmed. Tears rolled down my cheeks as I slowly put my socks and shoes back on.

It has been 20 years since I had my feet washed on that night. It was only just recently, after Holy Thursday of this year, that I fully understood the passage in the Bible, the experience that I had that night, and its implications for my life. In the passage in the Bible describing the Washing of the Feet, Jesus says:

> "If I, therefore, the master and teacher, have washed your feet,
> you ought to
> wash one another's feet. I have given you a model to follow,
> so that as I have
> done for you, you should also do. Amen, amen I say to you,
> no slave is greater
> than his master nor any messenger greater than the one who sent him."[1]

The implications of this statement are twofold. First, no one is more important than another, and second, we are here to serve one another. I have been looking for my unique path of service for a long time. Even after obtaining a Ph.D. and working as a college professor, I have felt dissatisfied and unfulfilled. The question that I have heard in the back of my mind for many years has been: "What is my life purpose?" Deep inside my heart I know what it is. I have seen glimpses. However, fears and limiting beliefs have gotten in the way far too long.

Jesus alluded to this as he replied to Peter, who wanted Jesus to not only wash his feet but also his hands and head, "Whoever has bathed has no need except to have his feet washed, for he is clean all over." [1] Thus a whole person is not "unclean" or "bad." There are only parts that get "dirty," and these are the only parts that need to be cleansed. When I was able to "wash away" the limiting beliefs and fears that were keeping me from following my own unique path of service and of being my purpose, the heaviness in my heart lifted and doors to my path of service opened wide.

We stand on our feet. Therefore, I invite you to take a look at what you stand for.

- Are your values aligned with your service, your life purpose, and your business?
- Is it time to take inventory of the "dirt" that you have been carrying around?
- Have you closed your heart to your dreams and hopes?
- Have you let limiting beliefs and fears determine your business?
- Have resentment and negative feelings towards others and yourself made your heart heavy?
- Have unworthiness and undeserving feelings paralyzed your efforts to follow your true path of service in order to have the life of your dreams?

If the answer to any of these questions is, "Yes," it is time for the "washing of the feet." It may take commitment and hard work, but you don't have to do it alone.

- Imagine doing what you love to do and getting paid for it!
- Imagine doing work that feels like play.
- Imagine feeling fulfilled and on purpose.
- Imagine living the life of your dreams.

The rewards are worth it!

LUZ LILIANA GARCIA, PH.D., is a scientist, professor of chemistry, licensed psychotherapist, art therapist, spiritual advisor, public speaker, writer, and workshop leader. Liliana powerfully and intuitively guides individuals on their journey to enlightenment so they can experience Divine wisdom, tune in to their life purpose, and heal their emotional pain. Visit www.TheArtOfEnlightenment.com to get your FREE copy of Liliana's special report, *"7 Steps to Enlightenment – How to Create Your Heaven on Earth."*

[1] The New American Bible, Catholic Bible Press, Nashville, 1987. John 13 (1-20).

Eliminate SABOTAGE:
Be a Manifestation Machine!

C H R I S T I N E   M .   L O N G

Hands up – who wants abundance? That's like asking a three-year-old if they would like ice cream on a summer's day.

Do you struggle with success, resulting in a never-ending cycle of lack and discontentment? Do you create abundantly, yet do not feel fulfilled?

You are your own personal foundation, the absolute bottom line of what happens regarding your success. Where the gaps or cracks are within you is where your capacity to create abundantly is diluted. It is amazing how many entrepreneurs do not heed this fact and wonder why they often feel burnt out, disillusioned, or discontent with their lot, with no life raft in sight.

It is essential that your emotional and mental state, along with your spiritual self, all interact and communicate with each other. **Without this level of awareness and alignment, you cannot expand or succeed with the depth of fulfillment that the "whole" you naturally resonates to and innately desires.**

The following **eight effective Eliminate SABOTAGE strategies** will shift your physical well-being, mindset wisdom, emotional intelligence, and spiritual essence.

STEP 1		STEP 2		OUTCOME
SELF-CARE	⇨	Strength	⇨	Solace
ATTITUDE	⇨	Acceptance	⇨	Authenticity
BOTTOM-LINE	⇨	Build	⇨	Buoyancy
OBJECTIVE	⇨	Oversee	⇨	Opportunity
TEMPERANCE	⇨	Tenacity	⇨	Trust
ACTION	⇨	Allow	⇨	Attraction
GRATITUDE	⇨	Growth	⇨	Guts
ENTHUSIASM	⇨	Expansion	⇨	Empowerment

STRATEGY 1

SELF-CARE ⇨ Strength ⇨ Solace

Would you recommend to the dearest and closest person to you that they treat themselves the way you treat yourself? This is an excellent gauge for measuring how well you look after you. Taking care of your health and well-being can sound time-consuming, boring and self-obsessed. But when you are not caring for yourself, what do you think this is telling your mind, body, and soul, and the external world?

The message is loud and clear. It is saying: "I do not want my needs, wants, and desires fulfilled. This includes everything that takes care of me abundantly." Ouch!

If any area of you is neglected on an ongoing basis, it will only be a matter of time before your manifestation ability is quashed. Therefore find what **specifically suits you,** so you can actually enjoy the process and draw to you more of what does fulfill you.

When you don't take care of the necessary resources within you, you are unable to function in a powerfully-aligned manner, and SELF-SABOTAGE is the result. Therefore, appreciate your body, expand your mind, honor your emotions, respect your spiritual essence, and generously donate to your own **"Self-Care Foundation."**

STRATEGY 2

ATTITUDE ⇨ Acceptance ⇨ Authenticity

The word "authenticity," when related to an individual, has a depth of meaning that is often not understood. It encompasses all aspects of a person and how they live and "be" in every aspect of their life.

How would you feel if you knew that you were "bona fide," "valid," the "real deal," the "genuine item?" Would that put a spring in your step and give you permission to break free? How cool would it be to feel 100% congruent with the "real you?" This is where your treasure trove of gifts, talents, and skills reside, where you true identity thrives. Why not give yourself a stamp of approval, live what this represents every day, and watch the magic unfold?

Being who you truly are is contagious and influences all those with whom you interact. You then experience firsthand other people's authenticity, and that's when the "WOW" factor becomes your reality and sabotages fall away into pale insignificance.

STRATEGY 3

BOTTOM-LINE ⇨ Build ⇨ Buoyancy

The Bottom-line referred to here is actually your owning what is happening within you on any level at any time, whether it be mentally, emotionally, physically, or spiritually. This is not an exercise you perform, it's actually a state of being. Without doing this kind of reality check you may build on shaky ground.

Due diligence in implementing this behavior is crucial for you to fill in the cracks (if any) and, preferably, to avoid their appearing in the first place. When you are crystal clear about you, you possess a deep sense of resilience when situations become challenging, which they do when breaking through new ground. If you don't master you, you can fall prey to your ego, or be in denial, and your ability to manifest and create abundantly will be diminished.

STRATEGY 4

OBJECTIVE ⇨ Oversee ⇨ Opportunity

Do you find yourself drawn into what is happening to everyone around you? Did you know that what is happening outside of yourself is none of your business? Now, that statement may have put you into a "but" or defense mode, so allow me to explain. When you are clear about you, this clarity provides the focus required to attain your true heart's desires. Of course you address situations that are presented to you and enjoy your interactions with others. However, the more focused you are about being clear yourself (not just in your mind – this strategy is about embracing the whole you), the more your objectivity is enhanced and the gift to oversee successfully is the result. This creates more and more opportunity that is in alignment with you and your desires.

Allow yourself to be connected to yourself and in so doing, you will bond with others on a higher level that manifests powerful, abundant outcomes for all.

STRATEGY 5

TEMPERANCE ⇨ Tenacity ⇨ Trust

Trust what? Trust who? The good news is that this is about trusting yourself. When you know that you are there for yourself no matter what, you are instantly your most powerful ally and friend.

I am not suggesting you operate as if you are on a deserted island, as the enjoyment of working, interacting, and playing with others can bring much pleasure and satisfaction. However, it is crucial that you acknowledge the importance of yourself in every endeavor, and understand your profound impact on whatever is being created around you.

This is quite different from a sabotage mindset, in which you think you need external help because you don't trust you. This sabotage way of operating attracts people who are not suitable to assist you – who end up doing the very thing you are trying to avoid. When you have the temperance to discern your priorities, the tenacity to implement them, and the trust to seek assistance when appropriate, a powerful dynamic is formed that manifests instant and long-term results.

An unfaltering commitment to yourself will give you the temperance and tenacity to be the Manifestation Machine that works for you and not against you.

STRATEGY 6

ACTION ⇨ Allow ⇨ Attraction

Do you say to yourself, "I would really like to have this," or "I would really like to do that?" Well, what's stopping you? Is this when excuses reveal themselves? The Law of Attraction approach suggests that you take action by implementing simple steps, such as Googling what you want to attract, researching, and talking and brainstorming with others for guidance, insight, and clarity. This process acts like a magnetic energy force, and as you experience the results of your actions. Allow the time and space for them to unfold; they build an extraordinary momentum.

You don't have to be an expert or know all the "how tos" – just visualize the desired outcome and the rest will be revealed when you allow it to flow and continue to act upon what transpires.

STRATEGY 7

GRATITUDE ⇨ Growth ⇨ Guts

When you are in a place of gratitude, your focus is on appreciating what you already have. How magnetic is that? Gratitude gives you the power to move mountains because it fosters optimism and focuses you away from fears about lack and loss. What a wonderful way to pass the time: feeling, knowing, and appreciating so much about yourself and your life?

Having the guts requires the knowing part of you to appreciate what you are and grow beyond your limitations of doubt and lack. This growth instills a deep realization of gratitude in which you flourish and grow and naturally manifest abundantly.

STRATEGY 8

ENTHUSIASM ⇨ Expansion ⇨ Empowerment

When they think about empowerment, some people think about demonstrating an assertive behavior to get what you want. What does enthusiasm do for you? What happens when someone you know is enthusiastic? How empowered and expansive is this state? It is like a brilliant flame that cannot be dulled. This energy is so powerful and generous that others can't help but respond enthusiastically. When the radiant effect of enthusiasm permeates you, it can connect you to people and situations in a profound way. Your empowered and expansive persona has limitless potential and your ability to attract abundance is immense.

Empowerment is what you already are when you are enthusiastic, and expansion is its natural by-product.

SUMMARY

To graciously manifest both success and fulfillment, you must acknowledge that your past affects your present and your present creates your future, while daring to explore and build deep and wide within yourself by using the above **eight effective Eliminate SABOTAGE strategies.**

CHRISTINE M. LONG, The Sabotage Eliminator, is founder of Australian Aromatic Essences – Formula for Life in a Bottle, and Inner Insight Mastery Intuitive Readings. These cutting-edge solutions clear blocks and are designed to assist you in living up to your full potential as they harness the power of your mind/body/soul connection. Visit www.AustralianAromaticEssences.com to download FREE the *Your Energy Matrix – Friend or Saboteur* audio, plus the *Heavenly Haven Music* audio, which helps remove resistance and regain resilience.

CHAPTER TEN

Your Roadmap to Success Begins With Alignment

LIANDA LUDWIG

Your life's work can be seen as a journey towards a wonderful destination of your choosing. Rather than sitting as a passenger in a car going nowhere in particular, you can choose to go where you've always dreamed of going.

Where is your destination?

Why do you want to be an entrepreneur? It's not an easy road for the faint-hearted! If you are a security-minded person who wants to leave the job behind when you leave your office, it probably is not a good choice to be an entrepreneur. But if you are spending your precious time going to a job you hate, and counting down the hours for your day to be over, you are wishing your life away. Your life doesn't begin on your way back home from work; it begins the moment you open your eyes each morning and greet the day.

There are two distinctly different roads that you can take when embarking on the decision about work. You can find someone to employ you, or you can embrace what you love to do – your passion, if you will – and find someone who will pay you to do it! Which would you rather do?

It's important to understand your personality and your needs before embarking on the arduous road to being a business owner. Do you want to look back and see that your job was your occupation, or that you had a life in which your occupation was living and working at something you valued, that had meaning, and that you feel proud of? After all, you are trading your time on this planet for money. This is your one life, why waste it?

It takes courage to be who you are meant to be.

You are born equipped with your own unique interests, talents, and way of seeing the world. Your distinctive contribution can potentially improve the world in some way, be it large or small. That is your life's mission, purpose, or destination. Sharing those talents and gifts can be thought of as your moral responsibility.

If you follow someone else's map instead of your own, or take the path of least resistance, your gifts will go unused and your life will remain unfulfilled. Get ready for the journey.

You must first know your heart's purpose and desire, and where you're going! If you don't know where you're going, you may end up in the wrong place!

It seems obvious, but many people start a business without knowing where they're going! It's like embarking on a long road trip without making sure your vehicle is road-worthy! It's not enough to have a dream of where you want to go; you need a map and a solid plan. Wishes are not goals! You need to know your destination in order to plan how to get there.

The most important part of your journey begins with making sure your idea for business fits with your values and interests, and that you are in alignment with your purpose. This will make future decisions very clear, because you are operating with integrity. Imagine how your road trip would go if the wheels on your vehicle weren't aligned, but were all pointing in different directions! You wouldn't get far without blowing the tires and burning out the engine, because alignment is the "heart" of the car.

To assure your success in reaching your destination, use your heart as your compass for gauging how decisions "feel." To be successful, do what you love. You will spend a lot of time on this road, and you want to make certain that you are prepared for every twist and turn that leads to your destination!

Planning for a successful journey means learning about the potential pitfalls, hazards and roadblocks that may lie ahead. Only through excellent and thorough planning will you EARN the skills and develop the confidence to embark on your journey. It's great to have a wonderful idea, but taking off without thorough planning is a surefire way to get you stuck in a rut in the road.

Preparation gives you the confidence to start the journey. We live in a time when there is a great deal of easily accessible information available to help you prepare for your journey. Only when you have done your due diligence by investigating, learning, and interviewing those who have done this before you, will you have the information necessary to anticipate and plan ahead for contingencies. You will earn confidence because you are already prepared.

THE MOST DANGEROUS ROADBLOCK: FEAR

Yes, doing something totally new takes you out of your comfort zone. You have to give up something old to start something new. For some, fear motivates them to do something too quickly, without thinking, which makes them vulnerable to serious mistakes. Fear clouds your thinking and makes decision-making perilous. For others, fear can have a paralyzing effect, like being a deer caught in the headlights. If you can't move forward, all your hopes will remain mere dreams. You'll never move to the point where you start to see your success!

Instead, use fear as a signal that is telling you something still needs clarification. Distance yourself from the fear by doing the things that you know help you get calm. Take a walk, a leisurely bath, listen to calm and happy music, look at pictures from a happy time, do some stretches or yoga, talk to a friend, and focus on getting your emotions to a neutral gear. Then when you feel calm, re-think the thoughts that focused you on fear. From this place of neutrality, you can more readily assess the validity and reality of those thoughts.

Act your way into a new belief. Imagine the manner in which a successful executive might handle that obstacle. Yes, when you imagine yourself in a role, you "become" that role, even for a short time. It can bring new clarity and creative ideas that you've never considered before. Most important, decisions made in fear are not likely to be the best ways to solve your problems.

TOOLS TO GET YOU OUT OF THE RUT IN THE ROAD

No matter what your destination, be it a new business or a change in your personal life, getting stuck keeps us in a place that we don't like. If you use terminology such as: "I lost control…" "I can't help it…" "I should, I know, but…" it's important to realize that you might be stuck and need help.

"Whether you think you can, or you think you can't you are right."

~ HENRY FORD

Life is a series of choices. Every minute of every day we are unconsciously deciding how we spend our time and what thoughts we think, and determining our attitude. Even if you are procrastinating or "stuck," you are still making a decision that is saying, "I'm more comfortable staying here than moving forward towards my goal." It's important to understand that you have made a choice by not choosing! Once you accept this responsibility, it takes personal courage and commitment to move forward.

One of the most insidious causes of procrastination is the obsessive repetition of negative self-defining statements. It is imperative that you replace the negative self-talk that silently poisons your resolve to change and self-sabotages your ability to move forward. By focusing on what you can't do, or your fears, you attract failure.

You cannot stop these negative thoughts by saying, "I'm not going to think negative thoughts!" That's like saying, "I'm not going to think about a purple elephant." To attract success you must replace the negative thinking with positive statements. Affirmations such as, "I AM able to achieve; I am smart and resilient."

Affirmations are one of the most powerful tools to get you out of a rut. Scientific research has shown that affirmations can indeed change your brain's wiring, so that you can believe you are a winner. And believing is seeing.

Combining positive affirmations with heart/mind tools will strengthen your resolve, self-esteem, and confidence; the road ahead will seem much easier to navigate. You can trust that you've done the necessary preparations and are ready for practically any obstacle that may appear around the bend. And even if you didn't anticipate a problem in all your research and planning, you will be able to forge your own path using your heart as a compass to see the right way.

When you can see the road in front of you, mile by mile, your destination comes closer until you reach your goal.

"A journey of a thousand miles begins with a single step."

~ Lao-tzu

You have what it takes to reach your goal. Go now. Your car is waiting for you to turn the key and put your foot on the gas pedal. Have a safe, successful, and fun journey! Don't forget to enjoy the ride.

And remember, life is a journey, not a destination.

LIANDA LUDWIG, MS, author, speaker, and coach, lovingly reminds you, "In case of an emergency, put on your own oxygen mask first, and then help others!" A HeartMath coach, she employs meridian tapping (EFT) and affirmations for clients to attain well-being and improved health by living in integrity. In her FREE report on her website, www.Heartfelt-Stress-Relief.com, you'll learn The #1 Essential Factor to know if you're ready for relief and change in your life.

CHAPTER ELEVEN

The Reinvention of Me

JENNIFER SHAW

I stood in my front yard staring absently at what resembled my house. A June morning breeze sent a chill through my body as I remembered pulling in the drive the day before to the sight of smoke pouring out of the roof. From there it was a blur. Home alone, I rushed around rescuing pets that were in the house, moving mares and their newly born foals that were in a pasture too close for comfort, and frantically trying to call for help on a cell phone that had one bar left on the battery.

I couldn't help but wonder, "What is going on with my life?" Within the past year, I had lost my job, my mentor, and a very dear friend who was also my best client, and now this?

Then there was the pain in my spine and neck from an auto accident years ago that was causing me to participate less and less in my job and my life – a life that I loved as a farm manager and breeder of racehorses. A plate in my neck and severe stenosis of the spine had every doctor in town shouting, "Get out of the horse business."

Now, walking around in the rubble, searching for one salvageable piece of my life, I couldn't help but wonder, "Was the house burning symbolic of a life passing?" As I rebuilt my home, how would I rebuild my life? There was a part of me that did not want to change, but would rather rebuild my life exactly as it had been. Even though I knew physically this was not going to be possible, I stubbornly clung to life as I knew and loved it.

Anytime we lose something we love or that serves us in a positive way, we grieve for it. In the beginning stages of this grief it is normal to deny the truth, so in the next weeks that followed, I pretended that my house was just being redecorated by my choice and that everything was fine. I dismissed the numbness and pain in my arms and legs as "just a flare up" that would go away, and that it would be back to business-as-usual soon. Meanwhile, inside, I had this nagging feeling that was urging me to look a little deeper.

The work on my house had slowly begun. I had a strong inclination to have it put back exactly as it was. Since the house was built in the '50s, this was not very reasonable. After months of searching for identical pieces and parts, I finally gave in to the fact that this was not going to be completely possible. A huge wave of self-pity swept over me and held me captive for what seemed a lifetime.

Self-pity, or victim mode, is a crucial part of grieving. It is an indication we are giving in to the truth, as we feel sorry for ourselves. It is here that we allow ourselves some time when no one, including ourselves, expects anything from us. It is a protection that can shield us temporarily as we prepare to move forward.

Absorbed in self-pity I got very little done. Rebuilding the house went slowly and it seemed literally that the workmen were destroying as much as they were repairing. It continued on this way, me feeling life was not fair and the house looking sad in a state of disrepair. Both of us clearly were charred, broken, and feeling defeated.

Life continued this way for several months and the longer it went on, the worse it got. I was more unsure about what to do with my life than ever before. Severe stress caused more physical pain and it became increasingly difficult to make even the simplest of decisions. One day when I was going to town to run errands, I got to the end of the driveway and discovered I could not remember where I was going.

This was the FINAL turning point.

Right then, I became furious at everything and everyone. The emotions were flying. I yelled; I cried; I beat my hands on the dashboard as I remembered every piece of my past: baby pictures, old letters from friends, a special rock, all gone in instant. It was then, at that very moment, that I made one of the most important decisions in my life – a decision that would define my life from that point forward. It was the willingness to take back control. To shout "No!" at what the universe was sending my way and to affirm the possibilities that I knew were lurking just beyond reach.

And so began my journey into the world of entrepreneurship. My first step was deliberate soul-searching and research that led me to information about life coaching. It was with this discovery that I knew I was on to something. The more I read, the more my heart sang with joy. An incredible opportunity lay before me. Here was my chance to not only earn an income, but to do so helping others overcome the adversity placed in their paths. It was a win/win for me.

The question now was, "Will I step up to this opportunity? Am I willing to work through my fears, to learn to stretch myself and do whatever it takes to make a difference?" For me the answer was relatively simple: "Yes!"

Even though I was excited about my new profession, at times I was also very torn. After all, the horses had been not just my profession, but also my way of living for pretty much my whole life. My heart tugged at what seemed the end of an era. To minimize this, I asked myself the question, "What if the horses and my farm could somehow play a role in my coaching?" I kept asking, but the answer would not show itself.

I believe the first step in being successful in anything we do is to find the very best resources and education available and dive in. I enrolled in a fantastic coaching institute and at age fifty-two began my new journey. Along the way, by trial and error, I aligned myself with other like-minded individuals for support and continued growth, which has now delivered me here – working from my home, helping other baby boomers discover that their own lives are full of possibilities.

I believe there is a definitive process to go through that supports you in what happens on your quest to entrepreneurship. It is the process I used myself that I have labeled HEAL. It goes something like this:

H - HERE and NOW. This was a wake-up call for me as I honestly examined exactly where I was at that point in time. Learning to reframe my thoughts allowed me to be curious and open. Voicing the affirmation, "I am a life coach" was fearful, yet exhilarating. It prepared me for action.

E - EXPRESS your feelings. After that first flood of emotions, I found myself raw and sensitive to my feelings. I continued to express my thoughts about my new journey, both positive and negative. I discovered the release of these emotions was a great relief, which moved me to the next step.

A – ACCEPT. The practice of accepting my emotions motivated me into a stronger sense of control and gave me power to move forward with my choice to become a coach. The fire had scarred me and left me with horrific anxiety every time I left the farm. I battled this affliction for several years, but learned to just acknowledge it and then ask, "How can I use this feeling to harness more positive energy for my work?" The answer came, "By helping others that are struggling, too."

L - LIVE. I stepped into my new role as life coach and my journey is one of tremendous joy. Continuing to build my service to help others is an act of love. The fire was a lesson that allowed me a new way to prosper, which grows stronger and more creatively every day. It reconnected me to my inner self and aligned me with a purpose that had been lying dormant for many years.

I'd like to add that when searching through the rubble, I did finally find a piece of my past: a little tile my youngest daughter had painted in pre-school that showed a picture of our house. Though a little faded, it sits in my bookcase as a reminder of where I have been, and the question of how the horses and farm would play a role in my coaching has been answered. This summer I unveil a new part of the plan: "Through Horses Eyes," an in-depth journey about how our four-legged friends teach us to communicate.

In contemplating starting a business, I leave you with this thought: You DON'T have to know the "hows" if you connect strongly to the "why." The "hows" will fall into place if each and every day you live the "why."

JENNIFER SHAW, ACC, is owner of Jennifer Shaw Coaching. As an inspirational speaker, coach, and author of published articles both on the internet and locally, her greatest fulfillment comes from supporting baby boomers as they weave through new territory and experience the challenges and opportunities life's transitions offer. To learn more about Jennifer Shaw and download a FREE ebook on how to HEAL, please visit www.JenniferShawCoaching.com.

Believe in the Possibilities
of Your Dreams

JANE STRASSEL

I am happy and grateful for this opportunity to share my life story in this amazing book, Align, Expand and Succeed: Shifting the Paradigm of Entrepreneurial Success. I trust that I will be guided to find the exact words to inspire millions to look at life through rose-colored glasses and find the beauty that surrounds us daily when we appreciate ourselves and others and enjoy this incredible opportunity called life!

As I listened to Lynne Klippel's teleseminar (Lynne wrote a chapter for this book), I knew without a doubt that I was going to be one of the chosen ones. Do you know that feeling, that moment when everything in your life comes into alignment and you are sitting in the middle of it, knowing that everything you have done in your life has set you up for something incredible? Well, that was what happened to me!

As I tell my story, it is my deepest desire to touch you and tell you this: Everything you want and need is waiting for you. You just have to line yourself up with it!

The past four years have been an incredible journey of learning, growing and sharing for me. After 15 years of a great marriage, I found myself a widow at an early age, losing Mark, my best friend and biggest supporter. As I reflect on what has happened, I am so blessed and grateful for the life I had with him and the incredible opportunities life has brought to me since that time. I have no doubt that Mark is still a big part of my life as I am pretty sure he is helping me write this now.

From the time I was 20 I had many careers: a secretary, working on the backside of a racetrack, waiting tables, owning a dry cleaners, working in a hotel, in retail, and in banking – I did it all. I also had some home-based businesses on the side – as I am a true entrepreneur at heart. I was always of the impression that if it wasn't fun, it was time to move on. I never thought of myself as a leader or manager, but my bosses apparently did. I continued to be recruited and promoted during my ten years in retail. I never thought I really fit the profile of "manager," but I continued to have great teams who worked together to produce incredible results and, most importantly, to have fun.

When people have a life-altering experience such as I did, most take a step back and look at what life is all about. What is your purpose and how do you accomplish what you came here to do once you find it?

After Mark's passing, I was extremely grateful that one of my home businesses allowed me to leave my retail career and take time for myself to reflect on my purpose. I spent the first year on a spiritual path and reconnecting with myself. I will never forget the day about two months after my husband passed, of sitting silently in my house, not having the energy to go out. I felt so alone and uninspired – unable to do anything. I looked around me and saw a stack of books nearby, and on the top, covered with dust, was one entitled, The Purpose Driven Life, by Rick Warren. I picked it up and started flipping through it. On about the second or third page was a statement about committing your next 40 days to God. The most incredible thing was that it was signed by my husband and me. I absolutely do not remember signing that book, but I do remember that my husband had bought the book six months earlier and that we were going to read a chapter a week. So, I kicked back in my recliner, and many tears later completed it.

So now what? I had no idea what my purpose in life was or how this journey would go, but to date it has been an incredible one. Of course, you are blindfolded going through the journey one puzzle piece at a time, but when the opportunity to be a co-author for this book presented itself, I felt like I was putting one of the last puzzle pieces in place.

The next unfolding step was when my best friend introduced me to the movie The Secret. I poured a glass of wine, got comfy on the sofa, and watched it. I have always been a bit naïve, but even I was a little skeptical of this idea of creating your life the way you want it. Visualizing what you want and then having it come to you... I was not so sure about that one! However, I was in a place where I was ready to put it to the test.

My first call to action was to gather my friends and have fun making our dream boards. Most of my pictures seemed a bit unrealistic at the time, but I kept the faith that this was a big part of "Ask and you shall receive." To be honest, I really didn't even know what I wanted.

Now that I had my dream board, I started writing out my gratitude list every day, and reading and listening to anything and everything that was inspiring. I was always guided to the next book, CD, or person at the right time. When I didn't have new material, I would revisit my old collection and find a different message that I needed to hear.

The One-Minute Millionaire: The Enlightened Way To Wealth, by Mark Victor Hansen and Robert G. Allen, is a book that was life-changing for me. It talked about millions of ideas out there, and how we need to take inspired action in order to give back to others.

A few weeks later when I was in the shower, I had an idea. I knew I needed a team to help me achieve it, and within one week I was blessed with them. We worked tirelessly on this project, which was creating an online vision/dream board. We had so much fun creating this site. We named it Catalog of Dreams because our big dream was to help others start dreaming again by creating their own dream boards.

My first dream board made from our site was incredible. I had asked the universe for a job, written a specific income needed by a specific date, and within two months I achieved it. This gave me the belief that I was on the right track.

About one year later, I received an email from a member asking if she could interview me on her Law of Attraction show on Blog Talk Radio. I was ecstatic! Of course I had never done anything like this before, but I trusted that it was just the next step. We had a blast doing the interview and after the show, she called and asked if I would consider being her co-host every Monday night. I was shocked and honored even though I wondered what I would be able to offer. Thankfully I had learned to take chances and accept what was being presented to me. Scared and excited, this left me no choice but to say, "Yes."

Interviewing one great author after another whose stories were so powerful and impactful simply amazed me. It allowed me to meet incredible authors I would never have had the opportunity to meet prior to that, including Lynne Klippel. It was because of this opportunity on the radio show, and meeting Lynne, that I was invited to hear about this book.

I believe that because I aligned myself, got clear on my goals and dreams, and realized that my main job was to be happy, I have now created an amazing life for myself and those around me.

I continue to attract those things that I once dreamt about. I have many incredible, amazing friends; multiple streams of income; a beautiful home; travel to all parts of the world for free; a wonderful, healthy family; my own healthy body; an opportunity to be a best-selling author, and am on my way to becoming an enlightened millionaire as I truly enjoy each day.

I know that my husband, Mark, has helped me through these past four years and will continue to be there for me in spirit. We had so much fun during the 15 years that we were lucky enough to spend together, and I have learned so much since his passing. I am no longer afraid of dying and am excited to take chances living, to see the beauty in every single minute of every single day, to look at everyone through the eyes of God and see their perfection, to be grateful and happy so that I can shine my light on others, and to believe that absolutely anything and everything is possible when you dream.

JANE STRASSEL is the founder of Catalog of Dreams, a website designed to create your own dream board online. She has co-hosted *Master Your Universe* on the Law of Attraction show on Blog Talk Radio, interviewing authors such as Lisa Nichols, Tony Burroughs, and Gay Hendricks. Her desire is to inspire you to live the life of your dreams. Visit Jane at www.JaneStrassel.com for an opportunity to share your story on her radio show or website.

CHAPTER THIRTEEN

Are You Living a Lie?
How to Excavate the Real You

SUE PAPADOULIS

FAKING IT

My chest thundered as my heart raced at up to 190 beats per minute. Tears splattered across my "To Do" list. Dressed in a stifling corporate suit and killer stilettos, I felt stripped bare and brought to my knees. Dizzy, trembling, and about to faint, I closed my office door, clutched my keyboard, punched out a "Do not disturb" email, and then slumped on the couch. My life, The Great Illusion of Sue, was about to crumble. Halleluiah!

It had been some years in the making, this breakdown. On that particular day, the universe had decided it was time to shake things up. It was done with keeping up appearances while I lived a life of quiet desperation. There had been warnings signs, but I'd ignored every one of them.

My three-year marriage was over and divorce proceedings were about to begin. I'd returned to live in my parents' home, sleeping in the single bed I'd long grown out of. Physically, I was sick. Until then I'd ignored the frightening bouts of heart palpitations, at times even driving my car on the verge of collapse. And I was falling for a man who was completely out of reach.

ALIGN, EXPAND, AND SUCCEED

It was a medical emergency that sparked the beginning of the end of my "sham-life," as I liked to call it. This man had suffered a heart attack. He was in intensive care surrounded by his close-knit family, and I was sitting in my office, crying, and unable to contact him.

Things changed that day. I still went through the motions of my life – wiping away the tears, breathing out my despair, and ticking off tasks on my list – but there had been a seismic shift. The things I believed defined me – my corporate career, financial wealth, travel, and the decision never to have children, no longer seemed relevant.

To the outside world I was "successful." I had forged a great career as a public relations manager, backed by ten years as a journalist and news editor. I knew where I was heading. Yet now, aged 32, I was completely lost. If this was "success," I didn't care for it anymore.

The panic attack, breakdown, emotional collapse – whatever you want to call it, was a line in the sand. I had to walk a new path. But how the hell do you do that, when you're so far down the wrong road with no map to show you the way out?

Excavating the Real You

I want to share with you the steps I took on this journey to the "real me." In doing so, I hope to inspire those of you who are still deep in the trenches of a life that's not truly your own.

1. **The first step on your path toward authenticity is to stay still**. While I didn't know which way to turn, the best option was to take no action at all. With courage, I decided not to apply for an executive role that had virtually been promised to me by the CEO. It was a big call and one that frustrated and confused my work colleagues. Didn't I realize I was ruining my career? Yes, and it was liberating.

2. **Spend time just being, rather than doing**. I went for long walks and really looked at my surroundings. Studying the bounty of the gifts from nature took me back to my childhood and a life of make-believe and freedom.

3. **Write daily in your journal.** At first, it was angry wild scrawl, blaming everyone and anyone for my predicament, but then the anger subsided and I felt a creative tug for the first time in years.

4. **Investigate your creative side.** I enrolled in a university course to study creative writing. My teenage undergraduate peers amused and inspired me with their ferocious zest for the meaning of life.

5. **Find an outlet for your emotion.** I sought regular counseling, unloading a mix of feelings and slowly working through my tangled view of myself and the world.

6. **Explore your spirituality.** I attended different churches, reading the teachings of the Bible and exploring the connection I felt with God when I visited the white-washed chapels of Greece during my 20s.

7. **Realize that everything you resist, persists.** I was angry about some things, furious with particular people, but I learned that the more I fought and the angrier I felt, the longer the situation lingered in my life.

8. **Surrender with faith.** Patience had never been a strong point, but I learned that regardless of how eager I was for change and for situations to be resolved, forcing the issue would only slow down the process. I accepted that a higher plan was unfolding for me in exactly the right way and at the right time.

9. **With your growing consciousness you will make new discoveries.** For me, the first was that I wanted to be a force for positive change. Until then I had tried to weave this goal into my career, but without success. In my job as a news editor, I launched a "good news" segment in the hourly bulletins. The general manager laughed at me before canning the idea permanently. So, I gave up journalism for the more positive world of public relations, but it simply wasn't enough.

THE ROAD TO AUTHENTIC SUCCESS

My next discovery was The Big One. It was truly a defining moment in my life. I wanted to have children and be a stay-at-home mom. What? It wasn't an easy thing to think, let alone say out loud. In my mind, being a stay-at-home mom was giving in and not stepping up to life's bigger, more successful callings.

It took some years and more soul searching before the dream of motherhood was realized. Thankfully, when the time was right, my new husband and I hadn't left it too late, and we became pregnant almost immediately. My kineseologist described my state as "fearful joy." I was still terrified of the unknown and unsure how we would cope financially, but I just knew in my heart of hearts that it was the right thing to do.

Incredibly, starting a family was the precursor to a fabulous new career – that of a work-from-home-mom. I previously had ambitions to start my own business, but had allowed fear to stop me. I knew nothing about accounting, taxation, building a website, or the many basics I now take for granted, but faced with the option of returning to my high-pressure city job and putting my daughter into day-care, it was almost as if the universe forced my hand.

So, I took a leap of faith, resigned, and started a home business in my area of expertise – public relations. Ten months later, I had a six figure enterprise and felt inspired to share my newfound knowledge with others.

I've finally realized my purpose – and that is to inspire others to reach their own greatness. I do this every day through Home Biz Chicks, the ultimate resource empowering women (and enlightened men!), who work from home.

The journey from stressed-out executive with few emotional attachments to a work-from-home-mom with two successful businesses has helped me become a force for positive change. There's no more fight for success. I've realized that success is something that manifests quietly by itself while you're living life as the real you.

The man I fell for who suffered a heart attack? He is my husband and we now live and work together from our home in Perth, Western Australia. It's no coincidence that our hearts were physically and emotionally broken – his manifesting as a heart attack and mine as severe heart palpitations. Mending our hearts has been a challenging yet joyful experience that has led us on the path to prosperity, abundance, and a happy family life.

The great irony is that opting out of a "successful" life has resulted in even greater success on all levels – financial, emotional, and personal.

A BLUEPRINT FOR THE AUTHENTICALLY SUCCESSFUL YOU:

1. **Take the time (10 minutes a day is all you need), to be still and listen to your intuition.** You have immense power. You just need to give yourself the means to access it, and you do that by being tranquil and quiet.

2. **See fear as an opportunity – push through it and you will grow and expand your horizons**. Take the paths in life that challenge you, and you will soon see yourself in a different and more successful light.

3. **See "success" as a measure of how authentically you are living your life.** The feelings of true success come when you are in alignment with your inner purpose. Life becomes easier. Making money becomes easier. Being happy becomes easier.

4. **Find a time and place each day to nurture your heart and spirit.** Explore your creativity. See the gifts of nature. Give the universe an opportunity to work its magic in your life.

Online entrepreneur *SUE PAPADOULIS* empowers and inspires women (and enlightened men), to live the life of their dreams by growing successful home businesses. She is the founder of Home Biz Chicks, which provides step-by-step advice on getting started, marketing, PR, finances, the best mindset, and juggling work vs. home. Access Sue's video, *How to Generate Free Publicity for Your Business* (value $279), FREE at www.diyprkit.com. Get Sue's $79 audio CD, *Secrets to Home Biz Success*, FREE at www.HomeBizChickscd.com.

CHAPTER FOURTEEN

Discover Your Creative Spirit

INDIE WOLF

"Let the beauty we love be what we do."

~ RUMI

Monday morning: 7:09 am. I hit the snooze button again, as if that will erase the reality that I have to be to my latest j.o.b. ("just over broke"), by 8 am… again.

I promised myself I would never do this again – take a job only for the money, when I had no passion for or even interest in the work; take a job that had absolutely nothing to do with my purpose, that did nothing to create more beauty, joy or love in the world. Yet here I am, having broken my promise… again.

There had long been something within me that knew there was another way, a place where I would feel excited and inspired with the possibility of being truly abundant while doing what I love. I had even had a taste of success a few times, but then succumbed to my fear of… what? Not being able to pay my bills? Not being "good enough" to make a living through my creativity? When would I allow myself to fully commit and create the life I really wanted?

Most of us have been taught to design a career for "security" or because it "makes sense." No matter that there is something inside us screaming to be released – a creative expression that our souls are dying to share with the world. As a society, our reality of the creative path has been the "starving artist" – a notion that has been both romanticized and ostracized, and a lifestyle that is often avoided at all costs.

What is the cost of avoiding your creative calling? Renowned psychologist Abraham Maslow defined self-actualization as a person's need to be and do that which the person was "born to do." When we are not giving expression to that which is within us that wants to be expressed, the result is often a sense of being unfulfilled, intense negativity, and even physical illness. According to Sarah Ban Breathnach, author of Simple Abundance, "If we're unsure of our passions, we must continue excavating until we rediscover them, for if we don't find outward expression to our passions in little ways every day, we will eventually experience the spontaneous combustion of our souls."

That is how it felt to me, and how it still feels when I am ignoring my inner voice to create. It begins as a dull ache, and if I ignore it, the pain increases until I feel like I'm going to explode! Though I had been attempting to make at least a portion of my income from my creative endeavors for many years, subconsciously I was still buying into that insidious cultural pressure: "Why don't you get a real job?" But when the pain became unbearable, I couldn't ignore it anymore, and made the commitment to my creative life!

FIND YOUR AUTHENTIC EXPRESSION

The big shift that we are experiencing in the world is nudging us to redefine our values and learn to rely on innate gifts and resources. Even those who don't feel they are creative or artistic are looking for innovative ways to support themselves and their families. Though I'm not suggesting that you leave your job and make the leap into this new life if it isn't the right path for you right now, the truth is most people can no longer rely on the old notions of stability and security within a particular job or company, and many are being forced to find another source of income. You may not think of yourself as an artist, but you do have an innate creativity; a way of approaching life that is unique, imaginative, and resourceful. These qualities are of the utmost importance in moving forward during this time of rapid and massive change.

So, if you don't know what your creative talents are, how do you find out? One of the best ways I've found is to explore anything that touches you deeply. Strong feelings of joy, love, and compassion are perfect indicators of when you are resonating with something or someone, or are aligned with your true self. Also, notice when others compliment you, or come to you repeatedly for advice on a particular subject. Do people tell you that you make the best cookies in the world, ask you for a copy of a photograph you have taken, admire a scene you painted, or praise a necklace you made? Often those around us will recognize our gifts before we do, so pay attention to these clues.

When you do create, be sure to engage your heart and soul in the process, rather than over-thinking it. Create what YOU love, what YOU find beautiful, and not only what you think others will like. In this way your results will be an authentic expression of your inner spirit, and you will make your personal contribution to the world by sharing your gifts.

Be Courageous

One of the biggest hurdles for many artists is sharing their work with others and, especially, offering their work for sale. You may have some fear about being criticized, and not being successful. As we touched on in the last section, one powerful tool to ease these fears is to make sure you are creating from your inner spirit – the part of you that is not swayed by the opinion of someone else; the part that knows what you have to give is valuable.

It is also vitally important to surround yourself with people who appreciate your creative process and believe in you, even when you don't. When you spend time with supportive people, your creative spirit is nurtured, encouraged to grow, and feels safe and validated.

The growth of the internet has made connecting with people around the world extremely easy. Websites such as Etsy.com have made it easy to create your own online store and communicate with millions of other artists and buyers. In addition, there are services now available that make creating a shopping cart on your own website very user-friendly. Establishing a blog is also a great tool, as it gives you more visibility and a venue to showcase your personality, style, and process.

All it takes is the courage and willingness to put your work out into the world and give those who are looking for you and what you offer the opportunity to find you. This includes being brave enough to share more of who you are along with what you do. Your vulnerability is an asset and helps others relate to you and forge a much stronger relationship. Yet also remember there is such a thing as sharing too much, so use your own intuition to find the "sweet spot" between transparency and privacy. Share your wisdom and experience to inform, support, and inspire those who are drawn to you and you will see positive growth in your business as well as in the rest of your life.

Cultivate Success

What is your definition of success? Is it a certain level of income, or a certain number of events, fans, or sales? Is it feeling good about what you are creating, and knowing you are having a positive impact on others? Is it being able to contribute to causes that are important to you?

Only you can define success for yourself, and for most people it is a combination of these areas. And though money isn't the only – or even the most important – measure of success, in our world it is definitely a factor. When we have enough money to spend (take care of the necessities of life), share (contribute to others in need), and to spare (build a fund for future opportunities and challenges), we have the freedom to make choices that we don't have if we are living paycheck to paycheck or sale to sale.

There are many cultural messages about money being evil, unspiritual, or a symptom of "selling out," but money is energy as is everything in our experience, and accepting money for our work is simply an exchange of energy. If money is an issue for you, it is crucial to explore your relationship with it and to heal any old wounds and messages in this area. Keep in mind that the ultimate goal is not to have more…but to express yourself more, experience life more, contribute to the world more.

YOU DESERVE TO LIVE A LIFE YOU LOVE!

Believe in your worth as an expression of your spirit, and bring your gifts to the world. Each one of us can be a bright star for those who are searching for a new way, a better way, to create a life they love. When you share your experience, what you've learned, and how you've grown, you promote your work while also encouraging others on their journey. Express your gifts fully and you will inspire others to do the same!

INDIE WOLF is a Certified Holistic Health and Spiritual Life Coach, writer, and spiritual jewelry designer, with a passion for helping people access their inner source of creativity, wisdom, and strength. Indie is a member of several organizations including Braveheart Women, the Women's Small Business Network, Conscious 360, and Artists Helping Animals. Visit Indie online at www.IndieWolfInspired.com and receive FREE support and resources to help you turn your creative dreams into a business you love!

PART TWO

Expand

CHAPTER FIFTEEN

The New Wealth: Three Keys to Align, Anchor, and Shift With the Changing World

JENETH BLACKERT

Whether you are talking to neighbors, watching television, or listening to the radio, you see it, hear it, and feel it! The planet has shifted and is changing before our eyes. We've seen tremendous upheavals. Mega financial institutions are going bankrupt and many people with "one-dimensional wealth" have lost it all. The old systems are failing all around us, all around the globe. Many people feel they are in a tail-spin of chaos, confusion, and fear.

Are you feeling it? Are you feeling the world shift? How are you coping? Can you see these shifts as neither bad nor good? Rumi said it best: "Out beyond ideas of wrong-doing and right-doing, there is a field. I'll meet you there."

What if we could see a world ready to grow in divine order? And what if all these unfortunate events are created to wake up this shifting world? Wake us up, so we can step up and deliberately create a better, more conscious planet – a planet where we come together and serve and support one another as a whole – with our whole self.

So, where do we start? Is it possible to start inside? To start with insight and imagination?

In The Biology of Transcendence: A Blueprint of the Human Spirit, Joseph Chilton Pearce writes, "Physiologically superior to ordinary eye-seeing, imagination comes in from higher up the 'evolutionary stream' of vision... rather than the senses impacting the mind with imagery, as in ordinary seeing through imagination the mind impacts the senses." What he's saying is that "real source" imagination can be our guide – our guide to purpose, passion, and the pursuit of an evolved world. Let's connect with that "real source."

THE MIND – THE FIRST POWER – TO ALIGN WITH THE NEW WEALTH

As I'm sure you will probably agree, most of us allow our imagination to operate unconsciously and let our fears get the best of us. However, when we practice deliberate imagination, our inner world shifts, then our personal physical world, and then we see true transformation and greater transformation for ourselves and others.

Where do we start in the exploration of this type of transformation?

I believe it's best to start with a simple understanding that includes four functions of the mind and the four functions of imagination.

Let's start with the four functions of the mind. I like to use the acronym **T.I.M.E.** to remember them.

T   for our conscious **T**houghts – for example, "I should call Sue."

I   for the **I**mages that we see. (We'll go more in depth about this area in a minute.)

M for our **M**ental patterns and behaviors, and the habits that run us.

E   for our **E**motional responses to our thoughts, images, and mental patterns.

Now, what are the four functions of the imagination? I like to use the acronym **R.I.S.E.** to remember this one.

R   for the Random images we see.
I   for the Intentional images we create in our mind.
S   for the Spontaneous insight we have when we are open.
E   for Envisioning what we desire.

By understanding these functions we can gain awareness of what's really going on in our mind and of our subtle energy. This awareness allows us the ability to transform by shifting the images in our head. This in turn shifts our emotions, which ultimately directs us to make better decisions and create our life based on purpose, passion, and pursuit of an aligned world.

But how? How do we shift the images in our head and allow new positive emotions to arise? Let's look at a simple process for managing our images.

Close your eyes and create an image in your mind. For now, let it be a nice image, maybe an upcoming vacation. Notice the energetic space the image creates. Label this "image energy." For example, "Ahhh... a beach day."

Investigate the "image energy." Every single image has its own energy that gives it power. The meaning behind the image is what engages us and what disengages us – if it's not as pleasant as a vacation. All "image energy" has some charge. Some are coupled with intense anxiety and agitation, while others are full of peace and joy. Rate the charge on a scale of 1-10 with 10 for extremely intense, and 1 for very little charge.

Once you figure out the charge, you can give it a directive:

Directive 1: Let the image go. The highly-charged "image energies" are a little stickier. These are the ones that obstruct us. These are what I call Dragons: certain images of fear that are so intensely-charged that they take us into emotional turmoil.

Directive 2: For these emotional Dragons, imagine the emotion as an actual Dragon. Find it in your body and connect to it in conversation. Notice what happens when this conversation begins. Oftentimes the irritation fades. Once you understand the Dragon's purpose you can ask it to leave. This may need to happen several times. This is one of my seven techniques in my "Mastering Your Dragons" system.

THE BODY – THE SECOND POWER – TO ANCHOR INTO NEW WEALTH WHOLENESS

We have literally been conditioned to allow life to unfold with all our Rs – "random images" – instead of listening and choosing our thoughts, images, mental patterns (behaviors), and emotions.

I often joke and say that many people just need a new kind of eye doctor and it's me. I'm the eye doctor for their bigger mental picture of life. As the eye doctor, I have three functions to clarify for people:

Imagination: Increase the big picture for a bigger life for themselves and the world.

Clarity: Increase the clarity in the vision so decisions can be made in alignment with that bigger vision.

Focus: Focus is where the mind meets the physical body. Focus allows a person to come to the task as a "whole being." Or as they say, "This is where the rubber meets the road."

The body plays a vital role in transformation. When we become committed to a task, we type words with our fingers, we speak words through our mouth, and we take action in our lives to create. You know this.

THE SOUL – THE THIRD POWER – TO SHIFT IN THE NEW WEALTH

Buddhist psychotherapist Mark Epstein says that what makes a person resilient is "accepting the truth of impermanence." Hindu tradition would say it a little differently. It says the ego must let go of its need to control reality. When we align ourselves with love in the soul, solutions arise, spontaneously, to seemingly insoluble problems.

What's next? Now, I ask **you**, what's next? Do you perceive it as what's next to happen in this broken world, or what's the next present action for you to take? The answer is for you to decide.

JENETH BLACKERT is a strategic marketing mentor and an intuitive business coach. She has personally taught hundreds of individuals her unique principles and approach to conscious business growth. Jeneth is the author of several books and programs including *Seven Dragons: A Guide to a Limitless Mind*, and the upcoming chick-lit, *Life's Magic Seven*. Discover the Dragons that are holding you back – take Jeneth's interactive quiz online at www.Jeneth.com.

CHAPTER SIXTEEN

Tao of Business: Wisdom of Gramm's Teaching

GUANG YUE "SUN" CHEN

My Gramm was five feet tall and walked slowly on her "bound feet." She survived the invasion of the Japanese and the new world order that came with the Communist Party taking over China. Her skills and formula for living had been learned from my great uncle, an herb farmer and rural local doctor. After growing up around and learning the ways she was taught as a child, she carried on what she had apprenticed, namely healing others out of and for compassion alone.

My Gramm revered the virtues of tradition and quietly and devoutly practiced them, despite the wildly changing mindsets in the world and the government of China. As the communist government purged traditional ways and introduced the brigades of the "cultural revolution," China not only discarded tradition, but rallied everyone against all individualism. My Gramm recognized people's pain and emotional confusion and, at great risk, she continued her healing center, helping people to find the proven traditions of Oriental medicine and lessons of Tao. In her service, my Gramm not only preserved the traditional wisdoms of the ages, she eased woes people faced in the new times. She became highly respected throughout her village. When I asked her what was her secret, she would get out a small, old book and read it with her sure voice that I can still hear today:

"Reverence for all life, natural sincerity, gentleness and supportiveness are the four virtues. They are not an external dogma, but a part of your original nature. When practiced, they give birth to wisdom and evoke the five blessings: health, wealth, happiness, longevity, and peace."

My Gramm's book was the Tao De Jin. The name can be translated as: The Great Way of Virtuous Living. It was passed down from generation to generation in China. Though it was more than a ten-year-old child could really understand, through it my Gramm planted seeds of virtuous living and principles of a good heart in me. Over the next many years my spirit blossomed like a small and mighty tree seedling breaking from an earth mixed with rocks and reaching the blue skies of today.

Great wisdom is not always understood and appreciated until we go through life and suffering.

Carrying on the direction of early apprenticeships and being willing to continue to learn the lessons of those much wiser, we break through to the open air. Now, many years later, I have followed my Gramm's footsteps and am a healer. I followed her path and graduated from medical school in China and became a doctor of neurology. My family has always told me I have the smile of my Gramm. At first I thought the difference between mine and my Gramm's was that my smile was based on great pride, as I was officially titled "Doctor," but I learned with time that the smile came from my nature and the blessings ingrained in me from my Gramm, and that it really was the same smile.

As the political climate changed, instead of being against individualism, China entered into its more mature period and opened up to a new and different economic system. China encouraged citizens to be entrepreneurial and to seek wealth and individual success, and I realized that I, too, wanted to achieve my own success.

I was tired of my routine work life, working in the regional hospital in China, and felt helpless and unable to really impact people's suffering. Seeking a change, I opened a shoe-store while continuing to work in the hospital. For years, I worked seven days a week, fourteen hours a day, pursuing my new entrepreneurial direction to make money. However, I felt unfulfilled and I began to gamble, party and drink, adopting the lifestyle of success. I still continued to feel inadequate no matter how much I worked and how much I made. I continued to grow restless and depressed, caught up in the cycle of gambling and alcohol. I became more discouraged and exhausted.

I ended up lying on a hospital bed, diagnosed with severe fatigue syndrome and supposedly incurable health problems. Staring at the white ceiling, hearing liquid dropping into my body, my mind was blank with no thoughts whatsoever for many days. I thought I no longer had any reason to live.

As I lay there feeling hopeless, I heard my Gramm calling me. Her voice reminded me that I was too busy thinking about where I was going, and that I had lost sight of where I had come from. I called my Gramm, and her voice from the other end of the line gave me the strength to again believe that my life had value and purpose. I immediately flew to visit her and I stayed for the next two months until her 90th birthday. When I first saw my Gramm, she got out her worn out, dog-eared old book, the Tao De Jin, and read to me in the same voice of my childhood:

"The practice of the Tao involves daily diminishing; decreasing until nothing is being done. When nothing is being done, ironically nothing can be left undone."

Following my Gramm's voice, my mind began opening and my spirit lifted, and then from my heart popped out the question: "Who am I, and where am I going?" I reached for my Gramm's book, sank into the couch, and read with great hunger.

Day after day, I searched through my Gramm's book for answers. Not only feeding my spiritual hunger, my Gramm taught me the natural ways to gain energy and treat illnesses. I had not previously heard much of my Gramm's teaching, even through my years of medical school and my eighteen years of medical practice. I now felt the wisdom of her hopefulness and I knew that life is wonderful. Just to exist was not enough. Finding the purpose of life now became my quest.

I inherited my Gramm's Tao book, and I have digested it little by little every day since she passed away. My Tao studies have opened my mind and increased my hunger for a meaningful life and a purposeful business practice. I closed my shoe business, quit my job at the hospital, and enrolled in a Chinese medicine school to more fully understand the healing and wisdom of Oriental medicine that was at the heart of what my grandmother had taught me.

For years, I enjoyed a simple student life, and sought the answers from the Tao. I wanted to find the answer to my question, "Who am I, and where am I going?" Finally, I heard a whisper from deep within my heart that said, "You are the Sun. Go enrich your life experience and use your wisdom to help others suffer less." I followed this calling and struck out for America where everything is possible. I landed in California, far away from China, with empty pockets, speaking very little broken English.

I have learned that we all have great gifts inside of us, and we can find them if we make it more important than material desires. Discovering our own gifts is a long inner journey, and to present our gifts to the world takes great courage.

It has been very challenging for me to walk this path. I remember the days when I was frightened just to hear the phone ring because I knew that I would not be able to understand the foreign language, and of course, those at the other end did not understand what I was saying either! I was limited to only working with Chinese-speaking customers, but my desire to get past this and fulfill my goal of healing and helping people motivated me to learn English as fast as I could.

Speaking English was a basic living skill I had to overcome while also regaining an ability to make a living. I did all that I could to be able to use what I had learned to benefit others. I worked long hours again toward my dream of establishing a natural healing and spiritual living service in a time of pharmaceutical-based mainstream thinking. I took endless business training courses, learning both English and business at the same time. I nearly lost the essence of myself in all the accounting and selling required to run a business.

"What is the purpose of having a business?" I asked myself. "What is the meaning of my business, and how can I survive if I want to fulfill this meaning?" Again, I felt calmed when I recalled my Gramm's voice echoing:

"Heaven is eternal – the earth endures. Why do heaven and earth last forever? They do not live for themselves only. This is the secret of this durability."

I know my grandmother wanted to tell me that business is more than making a living; true business is about helping people to live – giving people the tools to heal themselves – not just treating them and temporarily relieving pain. Healing is about helping people to wake up their inner power to achieve harmony and vibrancy. This now is my business – my Tao of Business.

GUANG YUE "SUN" CHEN is dedicated to helping others live healthy and successful lives. After 28 years in practice as a neurologist in China, and now a high performance coach and acupuncturist at Sun & Moon Wellness in San Jose, California, Sun has developed a unique program that bridges ancient mind-body-spiritual healing with advanced human performance science, bringing focus to the maximum potential for each of her clients. For more information please visit www.SunAndMoon-Wellness.com.

Broken Vows

MARLENE CLAY

By age ten I had made three vows to myself:

1. I would not depend on anyone for anything, especially money.
2. I would not show weakness or imperfection.
3. I would not get divorced, especially if I had kids.

Number 3 was the promise I did not keep, largely as a result of working so hard to keep numbers 1 and 2. I now look back at my childhood and have so much clarity and compassion for my parents, whose words and actions laid the path that ultimately led me to realize my life purpose.

I was six and my brother two when our parents divorced. My father remarried the following year, and as my stepmother took her place in our family, I felt my relationship with my father begin to slip away. My parents moved to different cities and my brother and I visited our dad every other weekend. My father often seemed frustrated and tense, and I quickly learned to dodge his anger and criticism by keeping quiet and staying out of the way. I loved to read so I kept my nose in my books as much as possible. Reading for me became not only a safety zone, but an escape from reality.

I learned to keep people at a safe distance.

I was naturally outspoken, confident, and active, but at my dad's house, the meek and timid, perfectionist Marlene emerged, resulting in my dad's belief that I was a very shy child. Because I didn't share much with him about my everyday life, he was often surprised when I won leadership or citizenship awards, or participated in activities with friends. His reactions angered me because I felt that if he knew me at all, the last thing he would be was surprised. Looking back, I know my behavior helped create the distance between us and prevented him from knowing me. I was scared for him to know me because I was afraid of being close to him. I didn't want to have feelings for him as I was terrified of getting hurt, afraid I could never please him, never get his approval, so I didn't try. I made up my young mind that I didn't care what he thought and that I didn't need his approval. My brother took the opposite route. He tried desperately to win the approval of a man who was unable to give it, and when he didn't, he tried to at least get his attention by misbehaving and getting into trouble. That worked, and I watched from behind my books as my brother's spirit was broken by my father's reactions and reproach.

I learned that being myself was not okay.

It seemed we were always walking on eggshells, attempting to avoid any explosions, until one day finally the bomb went off. My father and step-mother filed for full custody of my brother and me when I was nine. My mother was in graduate school full-time and we were living off of her modest savings. Now her nest egg went to an attorney in the hope of re-taining custody. I was terrified that I would be taken from my mother, and remember lying in bed making plans to run away if I had to live with my father and stepmother. I thought surely if I ran away enough times, I would be allowed to go back to my mom. In court, my mom was made out to be an unfit mother, which was far from the truth. Somehow she still won the case, and our alternating weekend schedule continued. It was a relief, but it also seemed to cement the bitterness and conflict between my parents.

I learned that people could not be trusted.

I was too frightened of my father to talk to him openly about how I felt. I knew my mother was barely scraping by and always worried about money, so I didn't want to make my father angry enough that he might withhold money from us. He had much more money than my mother, which gave him a lot of control over our lives. I watched my mom work so hard for little pay, doing everything she could to provide for my brother and me. I don't recall her ever buying herself anything during my childhood. But I do remember my dad promising to buy us the clothes and toys we wanted if we would come live with him.

I learned that I had to choose between love and money.

When I graduated from college and got a job with a top consulting firm, I didn't have enough money to buy the suits I would need to wear, and timidly asked my father if I could borrow $400 to make the purchases. He agreed, then sent me a letter letting me know that this was the last time he would ever bail me out, and that I had to sign an agreement stating when I would pay him back. I bawled. When had I ever asked to be bailed out before? Me – the honors student, captain of the basketball and soccer teams, loved by all my teachers, working at least two jobs all through college, always trying to do what was "right" – why could I not escape his criticism and blame? I apologized for being such a burden and I paid the money back on schedule. I vowed I would never ask my father for anything again… ever.

I learned that asking for help was wrong.

My brother and I were often caught in the middle between our parents, playing peacemaker or messenger, or having to choose between them in a disagreement. I remember my father talking badly about my mother and wanting to scream at him to "shut up!" but silently hating him instead. Every major event in my life brought up anxiety and stress, as I tried to figure out how to include my parents but keep them apart, and somehow interact with them "equally." Holidays and birthdays were always challenging, planning how to see everyone without anyone feeling cheated.

I learned to put everyone else first.

Two events occurred that changed everything: My father retired and my daughter was born, and the result was a complete 180 degree turn in my relationship with my father and stepmother. Watching them with my daughter has been a wonderfully healing process for me, a tremendous gift. I've been able to witness the warmth, love, and fun they share with her that I longed for all those years. And my father told me he was proud of me for being such a good parent…words I thought I would never hear.

I learned that people can change and that love resides in all of us.

When I decided to get divorced, I felt tremendously guilty and was worried about the effect it would have on my daughter. It brought back memories from my childhood, and I was determined to create a completely different experience for her. Her father and I committed to working together to provide the best possible environment for her to grow up in, and we've succeeded beyond measure. I know that my daughter's memories of her childhood will be full of love and support, including family gatherings with her mom, dad, stepmom, and siblings. She will remember us all being on the same side – her side.

She has learned that divorce does not have to break your family apart or create lifelong heartache.

This coming full circle led me to my new career as a divorce coach. I work with parents during and after divorce so they can have a more harmonious experience and provide the thriving childhoods their children deserve, because I know firsthand what a difference it can make. As a child, I felt powerless as my family was torn apart, but now I help children in that same position by helping their parents understand the impact of their behavior and learn how to communicate and collaborate effectively. This is my passion.

In addition to absolutely loving what I now do for a living, I have grown immensely through the process of starting and running my own business. It has brought up many emotions, beliefs, memories, and pains from the past. I have been forced to examine who I am, what I believe in, how I feel about money, how I interact with others, how I give, and how I receive. Repeatedly, my choice has been to shrink and hide, or step up and grow.

I have learned the following:

- Being myself is essential to living a life of joy and purpose.
- Trusting others, opening my heart, and being imperfect is liberating.
- Love and money are not exclusive.
- Asking for help and support is an act of self-love. Collaboration fosters creativity, trust, and a sense of community.
- Compassion and forgiveness are precious gifts.

Learning these lessons allowed me to finally release the past and break vows 1 and 2.

MARLENE CLAY is a divorce coach, "Family Redefiner" and author. She is passionate about transforming the divorce process from a costly battle to a cohesive collaboration that enables parents to provide the happy, healthy childhoods their kids deserve, while moving forward in their own lives with dignity and joy. Visit www.DivorcedHappilyEverAfter.com to get your FREE Divorce C-A-R-E Checklist and learn more about Marlene's divorce story and how she can support you on your unique journey.

CHAPTER EIGHTEEN

Asleep at the Meal

SUE ANN GLEASON

I have a tattered photo tucked away in a leather-bound journal where I record my ideas and musings. In the photograph is a stylish young woman standing in front of Niagara Falls, a snapshot of that brief period between oppressive past and beleaguered future. She's wrapped in a stunning leopard coat. This is the only picture I have of my mother looking slender, beautiful, and happy.

My mother was a baby when her parents immigrated to this country. They settled on the west side of Buffalo, the Italian part of town, in the midst of the Great Depression. Her education came to an abrupt halt in the middle of her eighth grade year when her mother suffered a nervous breakdown. As the eldest daughter, she was needed at home to care for the family of seven. Consequently, she never really had a childhood. And she certainly never had the opportunity to explore her intellect or realize her dreams.

A few years later my mother did what most young women did in the early 1940s: she married a promising young man. They had children, moved out of the city to a cookie-cutter house in the suburbs, and proceeded to live the American Dream. There was only one problem. That dream was not very exotic. The leopard coat was unceremoniously stuffed into a box in the attic, replaced by a shabby apron and a secondhand playpen. My mother's dreams ended up in another container. They were supplanted by the day-to-day tasks of cooking, cleaning, helping her children with homework she didn't understand, and stuffing her unexpressed (or, often, over-expressed) anger and disappointment with food, food, and more food.

I spent my childhood dodging her fury, trying unsuccessfully to earn her love and approval, and softening my sadness with food, food, and more food. I don't remember a great deal about my childhood, but I do remember my mother's rage. I could never predict when it would erupt, or what shape it would take – screaming, beatings, or excruciating silence. But it instilled in me a level of fear that permeated my childhood and seeped into my adult life.

It's no surprise that I grew up fearing angry outbursts. I avoided conflict at all costs. I'm still learning to speak my truth. The fearfulness, however, went much deeper. I was afraid to have children. I worried that, like my mother, I would resent the shackles of parenthood. Even though I excelled in my profession, I was afraid I'd lose my teaching job and end up on a street corner somewhere, but my biggest fear was that I'd become my mother – loud, large, menacing.

To compensate for all that fear, I became copiously compulsive. At various times in my life I've been an overachiever, a workaholic, a compulsive overeater, an exercise fanatic, and often all of the above. Those compulsive behaviors served me well, or so it seemed. I became an excellent teacher despite the inner critic telling me day after day, "You can do more, Sue Ann." I was very efficient. My calendar was color-coded. Even "spontaneous time" got a color – blue. I was proud of my resourcefulness. I was an accomplished multi-tasker and it even earned me the distinction of Teacher of the Year.

My teaching job, or rather, the way I went about my teaching career, kept me too busy to examine the anxiety, shame, and sadness hidden beneath my compulsive behaviors. Everything looked good from the outside. I jumped out of bed each morning at 4:30. There was no time for breakfast, but I did find forty-five minutes to pound the treadmill before racing off to prepare for my frolicking first graders. After school I was back at the gym.

The diets I participated in were foolish, but the exercise routine was becoming dangerous. My first wake-up call was a torn meniscus. No problem. I found the best orthopedic surgeon in town to repair the damage. He told me to stay home from work and rest the leg for a few weeks following the surgery. Instead, I sold my 5-speed Acura and purchased a car with an automatic transmission so that I could drive to work unimpeded by a clutch. It made sense to me. When my doctor discovered my automotive rebellion, he told my husband to take away my car keys. For the first time in my adult life I was forced to just sit and rest. My only reprieve was the bi-weekly trip to the physical therapist's office.

Something happened to me during that convalescence. I saw the way the sunlight danced through the windows as morning slipped into afternoon. I watched different species of birds take turns at the feeders, as the squirrels scrambled below, munching on the renegade seeds. I watched a clever chipmunk clean out an entire bird feeder in one afternoon as he fastidiously delivered one mouthful after another to his underground burrow. I read books. Not educational books. Novels. Memoirs. Poetry. I even watched a movie.

And for the first time ever, somebody brought me dinner – the biggest, most beautiful salad I'd ever laid eyes on. That simple act fed the child in me as well as the convalescing woman. I was beginning to see that my compulsive behaviors were really just strategies I'd developed to cover up a lifelong yearning to be nurtured.

For most people, a few weeks off with a bum knee would have provided insights enough. For me, it took two more diagnoses, one week apart. The first: "Sue Ann, your bone scan indicates osteoporosis. You can pick up a prescription for Fosamax at your drug store." And the second: "Sue Ann, you have Hashimoto's thyroid disorder. We've called in a prescription for you. You can pick up the Synthroid at your pharmacy." Surely, I thought to myself, these doctors will want to see me to discuss treatment options or at least explain the maladies, but alas, their involvement ended at their prescription pads.

Determined to delay the pharmaceutical train, I began a tenacious study of cellular rejuvenation through raw-food nutrition. I had literally been asleep at the meal. It became obvious that I was going to have to make some major food and lifestyle changes if I had any hope of altering the course of my health.

I started with my kitchen. A high-speed blender replaced the toaster oven. Flax seed crackers and raw food treats adorned the shelves in my pantry. Salads became works of art. I found great joy in sprouting seeds and planting a vegetable garden. I reveled in the vibrant colors and textures of succulent homegrown tomatoes, ravishing red peppers, crunchy cucumbers, and glorious greens. I no longer felt the compulsive need to exercise before racing off to school. Instead, I nourished myself with a green smoothie or fresh vegetable juice.

My passion to heal myself with food led to a new way of life and, eventually, a new career. First I studied nutrition. Then I went to culinary school to add yet another dimension to my practice — culinary nutritionist. I like the way those words feel on my tongue. My office is in my home. When I meet with a client, we first take a seat where the sunlight dances through the windows. It's a very sacred space. Then we move into the kitchen. I enjoy introducing my clients to the sumptuous nature of food. Once they experience the crunch of romaine lettuce or the snap of beans right from the garden... once I introduce their taste buds to the tantalizing flavors of freshly prepared, artfully seasoned whole foods, they seldom go back to packaged goods.

There's a line in one of my favorite songs by a gifted singer-songwriter, Shawn Colvin: "May we all find salvation in professions that heal." That's exactly what I've created. There were many gifts on this journey from childhood wounds, through forgiveness, and into serenity.

Not only did I reclaim my health and vitality, I no longer feel the need to reconcile the myriad feelings I have about my mother. Sometimes they're warm and full of compassion. Sometimes they're riddled with regret. The gloomy feelings always pass. I now realize they're just messengers that have come to tell me I'm driving myself too hard or falling back into old patterns that don't serve this new and radiant life. I don't own a leopard coat, but I do wear the smile of the lovely young woman in that tattered photo. And for the first time, I'm awake to every flavor, texture, and nuance of my life.

SUE ANN GLEASON, "The Radiant Life Expert," shows spirit-rich women and solo entrepreneurs how to nourish themselves from the inside out so that they can create a life that supports both their vitality and the growth of their business. "Dynamic Eating" coach, culinary nutritionist, speaker, and author, Sue Ann's unique "Fit, Radiant, and Rockin' Formula" has helped countless women reclaim their energy while growing a business that makes their heart sing. Visit www.ConsciousBitesNutrition.com to claim your "Radiant Life Blueprint."

CHAPTER NINETEEN

Lighting the Path to Self-Discovery

ANDREA HYLEN

This year, at the age of 53, I discovered something new about myself.

I AM COURAGEOUS.

For anyone who has watched the journey of my life, they might be wondering why I just figured this out. As many times as it has been mirrored back to me that I am courageous, I never really understood why anyone would say that.

I want to share some of the details leading up to this recent discovery, including the moment I woke up, how it changed my life, and how you can discover new things about yourself that will lead to a deeper way of living, as you!

Five years ago my husband died. Life stopped in many ways for our family. My husband was the main breadwinner. We were homeschooling our youngest daughter, and renovating an 11-room house together. When my husband died, I was thrown into action that involved selling his business and evicting a tenant who hadn't paid rent in a year, clearing unfinished projects out of a garage, and letting go of dreams we shared together.

During that same time, I was ordained as a Minister of Spiritual Peace-making, co-authored a book with 44 women called Conscious Choices: An Evolutionary Woman's Guide to Life, attended 78 Jonas Brothers concerts in 2 ½ years, and sold my house and all of its contents to move from Maryland to California.

Today I am in California with my 17-year-old daughter, living in hostels, hotels, and sublet rooms. We are on a journey of inspiration.

Now that you have some of the background, it is time to share the moment that happened just last month. I was having an emotionally painful week. We had been in California for four months and the foster home for my cats was no longer working. We needed a permanent place or a sublet that would allow animals.

I followed the spark of inspiration to look for a place to live and stepped into action. Every path I was inspired to follow ended with a door closing. I began to feel like a failure. I feared that maybe I would run out of money before I generated money from projects I was working on. Three days in a row, I felt overwhelming fear with self-talk that started like this:

"You are such a failure. You live in a la-la land of dreaming. What are you doing? Wake up! You are such a f**k-up."

That last line was the thing that stopped the mental whipping and inspired action to clear old patterns of fear and limitation.

"Stop it! Go for a walk. Feel the feelings. Take a look at them and let them go. Find the truth inside of you."

I would walk, feel the feelings, release the pain, and find a place of peace within me.

On the third day, something new happened. As I reached a feeling of peace, I felt my heart expand. There was a wave of love and compassion for myself. A memory from twenty years ago popped into my head.

In 1991, my son, Cooper, was born with a congenital heart defect. He had open-heart surgery when he was one week old. When the doctors told my husband and me that he might not survive the night, I decided to sit with Cooper and give him a message. With tears streaming down my face, I told my son that no matter what he chose, life or death, I would be by his side. I told him that if he wanted to fight for his life, I would be with him every step. And if living was too hard and he wanted to die, I would still love him with all my heart. Five minutes later the nurse told me his vital signs were improving. In this moment, he had chosen life.

I saw his courage. It never occurred to me that I was courageous, too. Wouldn't any mother do the same thing in the same situation? Walking down the street in Toluca Lake, California, twenty years later, I saw it for the first time. For 19 months, I sat with my son through two open-heart surgeries, a shunt, a hernia operation, and physical, occupational, and speech therapy. In the end, when my son was only 19 months old and was diagnosed with incurable fourth stage neuroblastoma cancer, we were with him as the doctor turned off the life support.

Until this moment, I did not see my courage because it didn't occur to me to be any other way. With a fresh perspective, I saw that it reflected my character and it was courageous to support him, love him, and stand by his side. My friends had been telling me this for a long time.

More memories flashed in my mind: leaving an abusive marriage, fighting for custody of my kids, homeschooling them, supporting my second husband in hospice, and becoming a conscious entrepreneur. All of it had taken courage.

The discovery came after a period of exploring a deeper connection to myself. I had been opening to inspiration with a 3-step process: Listen, Act, Receive. Here it is in a list of steps and ideas for lighting a path to your own self-discovery:

STEP ONE: LISTEN.

1. Listen to your heart. Create an environment of solitude through med-

itation, tai chi, or yoga. Focus on the love in your heart, one minute at a time, throughout the day. Breathe nature, art, and colors into your heart.

2. Play with the sparks of inspiration. Be open to curiosity and wonder. Listen to music that stirs your soul and lifts you up. Notice billboards, bumper stickers and books that bring subtle messages to you.

3. Keep the door of infinite possibilities open. Say yes and be willing to receive new answers to old questions. Journal a reflection of questions. Look at the idea from different angles.

Note: I added a new practice to my life a month before discovering my courageousness. I start the morning by connecting to myself for 5-30 minutes. I close my eyes. I breathe. I connect with my heart and spirit. I awaken. I listen in the silence.

STEP TWO: ACT.

1. Connect with your heart for action steps. Slow down, listen, and wait for the messages to come. Let go of the details. Move your body: walk, dance, swim – whatever makes you feel alive.

2. Get out of your comfort zone. Simple actions can lead to new ideas. Take little steps and big, running leaps. Do something unexpected to stretch yourself.

3. Observe yourself in action. Self-discovery and reflection in the moment is crucial. Make conscious changes to expand yourself. Process an experience with a friend.

Note: Recently I auditioned for one of Oprah's reality shows. The contest had crossed my path through personal emails from friends suggesting I audition. There wasn't a passionate desire to have a TV show, but I decided to move into action. Out of my comfort zone all day, I opened to the experience and stayed curious. I noticed where I was confident and where an old pattern of insecurity emerged. I made changes in myself during the day. After the audition, I was flooded with new ideas.

STEP THREE: RECEIVE.

1. Do an inventory of yourself. Where do you spend time and money? What dreams have you outgrown that are blocking the way for new dreams? Where are you placing limits on yourself?

2. Clear space for something new to emerge. Identify old patterns. Re-evaluate the inspiration. Let go of material possessions and be open to shifting in relationships.

3. Gratitude and appreciation. Embrace the journey. Be compassionate and gentle with yourself. See the gifts in all of the moments.

Note: Before you can receive, there is an element of releasing something. It may be an idea, a belief, a friend, a job, or a house. You can feel the spark of inspiration and take steps, but if you are still holding on to situations you have outgrown or have completed, there will be no space to receive the new.

This three-step process of Listen, Act, and Receive is an ongoing process to embrace and commit to for yourself. The connection to your heart will lead you to sparks of inspiration, action steps, and clearing a space within you to receive.

The gift of seeing my courage created a life-changing shift in me that day. When I saw that I was courageous, my courage grew tenfold. I began to look for more ways to be courageous. I started to recognize when I wasn't being courageous and I have become my own cheerleader, witnessing, encouraging, and celebrating myself each step of the way.

Now, when I look in the mirror every morning, I see what my friends have always seen. Looking into my eyes, I see an inspiring, courageous woman.

The journey continues…

ANDREA HYLEN is a minister of spiritual peacemaking, a facilitator for people in the ministry program, an inspiration coach, and co-author of *Conscious Choices: An Evolutionary Woman's Guide to Life*. Her next book, *Open to Inspiration: The Summer a Woman Discovered Herself with a Teenaged Daughter and the Jonas Brothers on a 10,000-Mile Road Trip*, will be published in 2011. Her greatest desire is to inspire people to live a deeper, richer life. www.OpenToInspiration.com.

CHAPTER TWENTY

Daring to Fly!

SUZANNE MASEFIELD, AIBMA

The feelings of separation and isolation I have felt at times in my life seem a distant memory as I present Nourish Your Soul to a seminar full of receptive people – as I dare to fly.

Sharing experiences of my journey from disconnection to inner collaboration, I recognize that the trials I have experienced have been a gift, teaching me more than theory alone ever could and allowing me to become honest, authentic, and compassionate with myself and my clients.

Growing up in England with parents and grandparents in the entertainment world, I was exposed to a variety of diverse experiences and personalities. On the surface people appeared happy and successful, but this superficial, ego-based world gauged people's value on what they had, what they did, or what others thought of them; a life view experienced in many areas of modern society.

The goal post of being good enough continually changed. It created a sense of uncertainty – a need to second-guess others with a feeling of being not quite right or safe. For me this led to an undercurrent of mild anxiety and at times escalated to heart-wrenching fear.

These feelings heightened my innate sensitivity and strengthened my intuition from an early age. This had pros and cons. It allowed me to read people and the environment and made me experience overwhelming emotions that I now know belonged to others.

As a child, I found this all very confusing. Knowing on many levels what people were experiencing, I found it strange when they often expressed the opposite of how they actually felt. This turned my inner world upside down as I tried to work out what was real and what was illusion. I had not yet learned to trust my intuition and was continually told to be quiet when I expressed a truth which was obviously quite embarrassing to the adults around me.

SEPARATION

I had little understanding of what I was experiencing on a conscious level and, since discussing feelings was not encouraged, I generally adopted the course of action my parents modeled: nervous hyper-action to move emotions (energy), suppressing or depressing what was uncomfortable, and shutting down a lot of my natural intuitive abilities as the confusion and resistance to them became overwhelming.

This continual trapping of unexpressed emotion ultimately led to major illness and my mother's hospitalization for several years, creating a breakdown within my family, forcing us all to face our own emotional demons.

Living without my mother, with a volatile father who just kept his head above water running a business and trying to manage four children, was an emotional rollercoaster of fear and survival. Being the eldest, I became the female head of the household, a role I was ill equipped to undertake. With both parents absent in one way or another, the sense of separation and abandonment was prevalent and my siblings and I created our own sub-family to cope.

Having too much responsibility and a lack of adult guidance at such an early age drained me. My school work suffered and, as my mother's illness was a secret, as things like that were not discussed, there was little support. Everyone did the best they could.

The escape I chose was a dysfunctional relationship and partying. I chose high-energy, action-oriented careers in sales, public relations in the entertainment industry, and then sales management in a UK-based American corporation. Knowing no better, I replicated the patterns I had grown up with.

My life was financially rewarding, incredibly busy, but unfulfilling. Something was missing... **ME!**

Living on the surface of life never really sustains anyone for long without consequences. My body took the toll of living a life I didn't want to be in, and I became physically and emotionally sick. I had to stop work and face myself.

SOMETHING HAD TO CHANGE – ME!

We all have pivotal moments in life when we get the opportunity to get real with ourselves. We need to take hold of our courage, step through our fear and the veil of uncertainty, take a leap of faith, and let our spirit guide us.

Although I felt like a failure, this blessing in disguise took me on a personal journey to uncover a deeper level of success that I could not have experienced following the old path.

My mother says we are good survivors and she is right, we are. But that has never been enough for me. I knew there must be more. I wanted to live. I wanted to thrive.

BACK IN TOUCH

As a means of recovery, I turned to counseling alongside alternative therapies. Becoming physically in touch, I marveled at how nurturing bodywork brought me home to myself. Essential oils and reiki healing soothed my mind and emotions, peeling off layers of the past, reconnecting my body, reawakening my spirit and my intuitive abilities.

Spending time with animals, as I did as a child, and getting back in flow with nature's rhythm helped free my spirit, becoming a saving grace, grounding and expanding my life on many levels.

COLLABORATION

True alignment came when I started supporting, collaborating and expressing the four aspects of myself – physical, mental, emotional, and spiritual – to live within the natural flow of life.

HONORING THE FOUR ASPECTS OF MY LIFE:

Physical – Exercising, healthy eating, quality sleep, nurturing touch, empowered action.

Mental – Positive self-talk, focused goals and plans, new learning, creative challenges.

Emotional – Conscious breathing, journaling, a good cry, sharing with friends, play time.

Spiritual – Meditation, music, being in nature, time out, gratitude, acknowledging, silence.

The results were amazing! My sense of powerlessness was replaced with a burning desire to learn more, to lead myself and others into experiencing positive transformation.

THE LEAP

Marrying a New Zealander, I emigrated in 1994 and set up a wellness business in Auckland incorporating bodywork, personal awareness, and growth. The challenge of leaving all I had known encouraged me to continue my studies in counseling. This guided my own personal transition into a new life, overcoming the disintegration of my first marriage and taking my work with clients to a whole new level.

Determined to succeed, I took charge from the inside out, faced the challenges and continued to develop practically and spiritually. I trained as a yoga teacher and mind/body analyst, and became a life coach. Using this knowledge of mind, body, and spirit connection in my own life led me to set up my business, Think Success Ltd.

Once I chose to be present with all of me consciously showing up in my life, my whole world expanded and flourished!

Working with clients over 16 years, I've found that when we leave out or persecute aspects of ourselves, we experience a sense that something's missing. We feel the need to fill that gap, often with things that fail to answer it – work, money, food, alcohol, shopping, toys, affairs, busyness, etc.

When our emotions/spirit/heart are ignored or not focused consciously, the ego naturally takes over to fill the gap. Nature abhors a vacuum!

When we run our lives or business from the ego, our success or failure are defined externally and often outside of our control. This creates underlying fear and a sense of powerlessness, breeding a need to tightly control our lives. Most of the world runs this way, with people and businesses often existing on a surface level, limiting the possibility of full potential.

RESPONSE-ABILITY

People become more and more discontent with the superficial goals they achieve because they leave their life aspirations unfulfilled. Many truly successful people are now choosing to take conscious control of their lives, developing integral collaboration within, with a willingness to extend this to working partnerships in business.

When we stop cutting off parts of ourselves to fit in with misconceived views of the right way to do it or what others think, and come home to our natural way of being, we create a heartfelt collaboration that shines out into our world.

I have witnessed the power of integral collaboration in my life and the lives of my clients, generating greater success and abundance on many levels.

COLLABORATION WITHIN CREATES COLLABORATION AND SUCCESS WITHOUT!

True success is not a linear process; it's nature's journey, ebbing and flowing as the seasons. Riding the rollercoaster of life wearing a seat belt of awareness, enjoying the peaks and learning from the dips, is a choice we make every day.

My mother's courage to survive and my tenacity to learn helped me honor the past and take charge of my life to use my experiences to **work for me** to thrive.

When we stop blaming and choose to take responsibility to be in flow with who we truly are, incorporating every aspect of ourselves, focusing on what we can do, instead of on areas we have no control over (ego-centered), then we stop reacting and positively respond (response-ability), to life, expanding our horizons to dare to fly.

The journey starts with you!

SUZANNE MASEFIELD is director of Think Success Ltd., an ICF executive coach, an AIBMA mind/body analyst, a clinical hypnotherapist and a reiki master. With 16 years' experience as an empowerment facilitator, inspirational speaker and writer, she facilitates "conscious leadership" with clients worldwide. The "Synergy Effect" inspires you to take conscious leadership of life personally and professionally, generating core level success – dare to fly! For free reports on self-belief strategies or managing fears, visit www.ThinkSuccess.co.nz and email Suzanne.

CHAPTER TWENTY ONE

What Would You Do If You Knew You Could Not Fail?

MICHELE MATTIA

"Why are you scared of something you don't even know is gonna happen?" Leila asked, in all of her five-year-oldness, with clenched hands on her hips and a look of confusion on her face.

It was the summer of 2006 and several of us had gathered at a friend's house for a barbeque. His backyard was expansive with many tall trees; however, the very best one of all had a tire swing. When Leila and her family arrived, she zeroed in on that tire swing long before the door to her parents car slammed shut. Out of all the people she could have asked to push her in this swing, Leila came to me, which would normally be a wise choice, but on this occasion I said no with a long list of whys. "The rope could snap, you could sail through the middle of the tire, and you could get hurt." She focused on my face for several minutes before throwing her hands up in the air and saying, "Oh well, I guess you're gonna be missing out on a lot of fun."

As you can imagine, Leila's words stuck with me. First, it was rather frustrating knowing a five-year-old was more connected to her spirit than I felt at age 37. Second, she was correct. I was no longer having fun in any areas of my life. Although at the time I had owned a successful technology consulting firm in Manhattan for close to a decade, lived in a fabulous Upper West Side apartment with views of Central Park, and travelled extensively, there was something missing. My divine plan and life purpose weren't anywhere to be found, but then again, up until that point I had not been looking very hard.

It was right then that I embraced the importance of my "life's dash" – the precious time between arrival and departure from this world that many of us take for granted. I took a good hard look at mine and knew I was no longer doing or living what I loved. I knew my life's dash was meant for something greater.

What happened next was, to date, the most anxiety-filled time in my life. I attended a silent retreat during a snowy February in Connecticut. Up until that point, the amount of silence I had experienced in my life could have fit into a thimble, but I knew if I didn't shut up and shut out my ego, I would not hear the still, small voice guiding me.

My anxiety was pretty high. I was not only putting my needs first, something foreign to me, but I feared discovering something that would require leaving my comfortable, safe, and secure lifestyle.

While on retreat, I had many opportunities to participate in walking meditations – a serene and solitary 30 minutes of crunching through snow with the smell of crisp winter air and snowflakes tickling my eyelashes. Prior to one of those walks, I asked myself this question: "What would you do right now if you knew you could not fail?" Within minutes, I came across a magnificent tree. Her limbs branched outward as if waiting to receive a hug from me and snow clung to tiny green leaves. It was the dead of winter and this was the only tree with foliage. For me it represented strength, growth, and limitless possibilities.

When I got back to the retreat center and sat in front of the fireplace, images of my tree and the words "life design," transformation, growth, creativity, abundance, prosperity, and coaching swirled in my head. I wrote in my journal "What are you thinking? Who leaves the success and security of an established company to start over based on a 30-minute walk?" But I knew I didn't love my current business and believed in my heart that we are not only meant to do what we love, but to live a life rich in joy, abundance, and prosperity while doing so.

By the end of the retreat, I had my company name and had designed the logo and written my mission statement: To inspire, co-create and support all of the possibilities people are courageous enough to demand. I knew what I wanted and now it came time to figure out how I was going to get my message out to the world, become a part of the conversation, and make a difference. My Life Design coaching practice would be more than the creative strategies I formulated with individuals and companies. I wanted to provide value, give back, connect, and collaborate with others.

I believe we are living in and experiencing a time when the rules we've known and mastered regarding work, career, entrepreneurship, partnership and networking have been altered. A job is no longer defined by a 9 am – 5 pm workday, nor does it have to be Monday to Friday. When choosing a career path or developing a startup, we aren't restricted to any one industry, geographic area, or position. More and more I see the fear of working in collaboration and cooperation with other individuals or companies dissipating because we understand that there is more than enough to go around, and being part of something bigger than ourselves not only makes a difference in our lives, but in the lives of others as well. The ever-evolving technology industry has fostered the growth of a global community, and one of the greatest resources we have as entrepreneurs is social networking. It's not about tactic or strategy, isolationism or the loss of the human connection. Social media embraces expansion, engagement, connection, and conversation. This valuable vehicle provides tremendous opportunity to learn from one another and effect change.

As I wrote the business and marketing plans for my new endeavor, social media became a prominent component. Transparency, honesty, and sincerity were high on my list of concepts, as well as developing an authentic voice and generating a brand through which people could see, feel and understand my message even if they had not yet met me in person. I was interested in what others had to say about the world they lived in, and if sharing my observations, philosophies and experiences inspired someone else to act or improve a situation, then my life purpose was on target. Additionally, it was important for me to incorporate my unique gifts, talents, and skills. I asked myself key questions like, "What comes naturally to you?" and "What makes your heart sing?" Knowing, honoring and incorporating the "who" I was into my company made the process all the more exciting.

Aside from my website, I immediately set up Twitter and LinkedIn presences, a Facebook Fanpage, and a blog, which connected with my passion for writing. From a very young age, I knew my words, whether spoken or written, were meant to heal and motivate. I remained centered on my desire for giving back and knew that not everyone would be able to afford my services. While meditating one morning, the idea of an eNewsletter manifested itself. I named it "Michele's Daily Dash – Words to inspire, support and motivate the creation of your empowered and dynamic life design." It would incorporate the blog I wrote Monday to Friday, affirmations, quotes, daily challenges, questions of the day, and topics that cover life, career, and business.

On more than one occasion I had people offering unsolicited commentary regarding my "Giving away the farm and not receiving compensation." Resolute in my absolute truth, the knowing that I'm making a difference in the lives of others and connecting like-minded people via my social networks in the hopes of their future collaboration was my compensation.

Within three months of the official start, the direction of my company was altered. Doing what I loved and becoming a part of a global community provided me with numerous occasions to meet and collaborate with people from all walks of life. Areas I had not thought to include in my practice showed up as opportunities and instead of worrying about the "how" of the situation, I stepped out on faith and answered, "YES!" I was asked to speak publicly at events, conferences, and on radio, and realized that my heart sang when I engaged audiences and began conversations that challenged perceptions, centered on living our absolute truth, and created dynamic and delicious lives.

The scared woman who feared that listening to and following her heart's guidance would lead to a significant lifestyle change was indeed correct. And she wouldn't change a thing! Every morning I wake up with a smile on my face and express gratitude for all the good I have in my life and all that will show up. Although entrepreneurship is hard work, when your business is a product of divine love, joy, giving back, allowing good to enter, setting daily intentions of positivity and saying yes to experiences, the hard work feels effortless. By living what I love, I have manifested my divine plan for becoming a part of the conversation and making a difference. I am grateful!

MICHELE MATTIA, a coach, creative strategist, writer, and inspirational speaker, founded Life Design after answering the question: "What would you do now if you knew you could not fail?" Specializing in areas of life, career and business, her mission is to inspire, support, and co-create all possibilities her clients are courageous enough to demand. To receive Michele's Daily Dash, an empowering eNewsletter and blog, go to www.DesigningYourDash.com. We are all meant to live dynamic lives!

CHAPTER TWENTY TWO

Business Bliss: The Sacred Path of the Spiritual Entrepreneur

EDWARD MILLS

"Nothing is more important than reconnecting with your bliss. Nothing is as rich. Nothing is more real."

~ DEEPAK CHOPRA

Do you remember the last time you moved? There is a moment when you have left your old home, but not yet settled in to your new one – a moment of excitement and anticipation as you begin creating your new vision of home. But this moment is also filled with stress and trepidation as you leave behind what is known and step into the unknown.

Beliefs are like our homes: You can rearrange them like your furniture. You can spruce them up with a good scrubbing and some new paint. You can even renovate your beliefs – tear down walls, add rooms, build a deck. But there are times in your life when no amount of work on your existing beliefs feels right. No amount of painting, rearranging, or renovating your beliefs can take you where you are being called: You are moving into a new belief system, a true paradigm shift.

As you make this shift, you enter a netherworld between the belief you are leaving and the one you are moving into. It is a type of purgatory where you are cleansed and made ready to enter the new world. The temptation can be strong to retreat back into the comfortable and safe environment you know, but you also recognize that your evolution is calling you forward into that new world.

That's the beautiful and uncomfortable place I was in while writing this chapter. My heart was leading me into a new world, urging me to write from a fully-embodied place of deep creativity and abundance. My head wanted me to stay safely entrenched in the old world, viewing this chapter as an opportunity to provide value, promote my business, and ultimately make more money.

My internal alignment was off. The writing was disconnected from my old belief system and not yet anchored in the new one. So, like a slightly off-key harmony in a song, the words fell flat and felt hollow.

As spiritual entrepreneurs, we are, collectively, in a similar and similarly uncomfortable place. We have started to let go of the old belief systems about business, but have not yet settled fully into the new one.

CASTLES IN THE AIR

"If you have built castles in the air, your work need not be lost; that is where they should be. Now put the foundations under them."

~ HENRY DAVID THOREAU

Some people seek to demonize the existing business model, blaming it for environmental destruction and societal degradation. As a spiritual entrepreneur it can be tempting to join in that finger-pointing. At times I have labeled business (and the business model itself) "wrong" when I see examples of businesses behaving badly. Coaching spiritual entrepreneurs, I often catch their unconscious and usually negative beliefs about business. Together we explore how those negative beliefs create roadblocks to their success.

As soon as you judge business you immediately cut yourself off from its massive potential power. Business has driven incredible growth, expansion, and evolution over the past 200-plus years. It has lifted huge masses of humanity out of the struggle to meet their basic needs to a level where they have the resources to explore higher, evolutionary desires. No other engine in human history has created such a shift in the dynamics of our global population in such a short time.

Henry David Thoreau spoke of castles in the air, and in many ways our existing business system is one of those castles. Without a solid foundation, it is heading for a crash. We've already seen parts of the castle starting to crumble. The financial meltdown is the most recent example.

It's important to remember that in evolutionary terms, our entrepreneurial system is an infant. We are just beginning to create this system and explore its potential. As with any emerging system there are many opportunities for improvement.

Think about your new ideas at the beginning of the creative process. They usually come out haphazardly and disconnected. You may look at your blossoming creation, which has very little in common with your vision, and feel the urge to give up. But that is the exact moment to build the foundation. Take those ideas – that castle – and solidly ground them into this physical world.

That's where we are in the creation of our entrepreneurial model. We've let our creative ideas flow. And what wonderful ideas they are! Yet without a solid foundation, nothing has grounded our business model in the physical world. That's why it has been so easy for businesses to disregard their impact on our world.

THE MISSING ELEMENT

"The earth is what we all have in common."

~ WENDELL BERRY

Contrast leads to desire. We look out at the world, see something we don't like, and imagine a possible alternative. This activates our desire, which inspires us to co-create the next iteration of the world we want.

While there is much beauty and good in business, there is also much contrast. Most spiritual entrepreneurs don't like the way some businesses disregard the consequences of their actions. And it's not hard to find examples of companies whose focus on profits has caused environmental and societal harm. This is a part of our present reality that we would prefer to change. We don't want businesses destroying ecosystems and communities. So let's explore what we do want. What can this contrast inspire us to create as spiritual entrepreneurs?

What if businesses focused their power on the renewal and rejuvenation of the Earth? What if the almost limitless creative energy in our business system went towards solving the problems of the world? What if the businesses that created the most positive change in the world also received the most appreciation, including monetary compensation?

That is the new business paradigm we are co-creating, one that embraces the powerful and proven structures of the existing system and injects the foundational element that has been missing.

That element is the Earth and the grounded sacredness that She models. We are here on this beautiful Earth and She will be our model, mentor, teacher, and co-creator in the process of building a new business model and a new world – if we let Her.

FOLLOW YOUR BLISS

When we look to the Earth as our entrepreneurial role model, our motto could easily be Joseph Campbell's famous line: "Follow your bliss." He said:

"If you follow your bliss, you put yourself on a kind of track that has been there all the while, waiting for you, and the life that you ought to be living is the one you are living."

The Earth is the ultimate "bliss follower!" She creates for the sheer joy of creating and is not concerned with the outcome. She is not focused on results – She is pure creativity.

As a spiritual entrepreneur it can be difficult to trust your bliss. Very few business schools or books teach this method of success, but we are creating a new model. The old rules don't apply, nor will they help us create this new model.

As you move through this transition, be patient with yourself and with the pace of transformation you see in the world. Neither you nor the existing business model needs to shift overnight. Remember: It took billions of years to manifest the old model, so be patient, but also have faith that when you do leap fully into the new world, it will catch you!

I've been experimenting with this faith recently, choosing projects based on my bliss, not on my bank balance. It's been scary at times, especially when cash flow is tight and my bank balance seems to be screaming, "Fill me up!" But as I move into the new paradigm and make decisions based on what feels "right," the money seems to flow effortlessly. Figuring out how it will come into my life is no longer a priority. I trust that when I follow my bliss the money will show up.

The decisions that come from my creative guidance often don't make sense from a business perspective. For instance, out of the blue I was hit by the guidance to offer a class on "Parenting from Abundance." I'm not a parenting teacher. That's not my niche. So, from a business perspective, it didn't seem like a good decision. Yet when I trusted that guidance and acted on it, it was one of my most popular and successful classes!

So, as we co-create this new business paradigm, begin following your bliss. Let it guide the creativity that wants to flow through you. For that creative spark will lead you to true success, which will help birth the new business paradigm.

EDWARD MILLS, author, coach, and teacher, guides modern-day mystics towards TRUE abundance, helping them discover and live a both/ and perspective that embraces their deep spiritual nature and the bliss of living in this physical world. Creator of the Abundant Mystic Telesummits, he has interviewed dozens of leading-edge thinkers including Marci Shimoff, Bob Doyle, Sonia Choquette, and Joe Vitale. Edward spends time learning from his daughter, making music, and dancing. For more information visit www.AbundantMystic.com/align/.

CHAPTER TWENTY THREE

SHIFT HAPPENS:
Inspiration for a Life in Transition

R. CHRISTIAN MINSON

A senior monk faced me in his simple ochre uniform. To me, however, he was more than just a monk; he was my counselor, my supervisor, my mentor and as close to a father as I felt I could have in the monastic order where I had spent the last ten years of my life. His counsel was compassionately simple and direct: "Then you must go…that is your Dharma, your truth."

I don't know how long I had been holding my breath, but the release flooded my being with a rushing wave of emotion and sensations of everything that was right. His words were a liberating confirmation of my own feelings; feelings that I had finally come to fully recognize only after nine months of agonizing consideration, counseling, prayer…and conscious breathing.

TRANSITIONS SERVE TO AWAKEN OUR POTENTIAL

Our conversation revolved around a decision of serious impact on my future: whether or not to leave the spiritual environment of the ashram for a new, undefined way of life. On the one hand was the familiar path to which I had dedicated a decade of my life – noble, predictable, comfortable, secure. On the other hand were uncertainty, ambiguity, and fear of a fast-paced, chaotic world from which I had been sheltered for the past ten years. It was like making a decision to leave my job, move to a new city, and get a divorce at the same time…with the added burden that the one I was "divorcing" was God (not that we wouldn't still be friends, but that I would no longer be living in His "house")! On the surface the choice seemed a "no-brainer." Yet deep inside there was a buried feeling compelling me to move in a new direction.

As all of us who have made life-changing decisions know, the experience can be traumatic. The territory is fraught with dark emotions of self-judgment, anxiety, anger, fear, and doubt. These days, as more and more people seek my assistance with their wellness, I realize that **to wrestle with these emotions during intense transitions is to be human. However, to overcome is Divine.**

In addition, there is every indication that the world is collectively moving towards a greater degree of change as old, unserving paradigms crumble and fall away and new, healthier, happiness-sustaining paradigms emerge to take their places.

Call these changes what you will – God's Divine Plan, the end of the Mayan Calendar, the inevitable effects of rampant greed and corruption – the times are calling for a shift. From a spiritual perspective, transitions are a natural energetic thrust to prod us into taking greater steps towards our truth, our authenticity. That means a lot of people are either choosing to make transitions or are being nudged out of resistance, sometimes forcibly, by energies that are calling for a shift.

THE BREATH – KEY TO ACCESSING YOUR UNIQUE TRUTH

The conclusion of my monastic journey revealed that I could no longer accept what outwardly appeared congruent while inside I felt out of balance. Ironically this understanding and the courage to leave the ashram came from more earnestly applying the spiritual teaching that I had learned inside the ashram! When I realized this I began to take what I had learned and transform it into something that I could share with others outside the cloistered grounds; something that significantly impacts the life of anyone who seeks relief from suffering. The simple elegance of the result left me in a state of inspiration – literally. The very definition of inspiration means "to breathe in." The secret lies in the way we breathe.

Using special conscious breathing techniques, we can connect with the most authentic parts of us, the parts that fuse passion and purpose into a fire of alchemy that naturally creates a path towards fulfillment of both. In other words, we discover our **dharma—individual truth in alignment with universal truth—our unique authenticity.**

My personal breath practice led me to understand that the longevity of my happiness relied on living three important intentions:

* I take personal responsibility for my happiness.
* I face my fears.
* I trust my intuition.

If the course of my life did not support these intentions, I would continue to be out of alignment with my authentic self and suffer as a result. Instead I have chosen to listen to my inner guidance and apply it in my daily personal and professional life.

Whether or not these particular intentions resonate with you is not of consequence. What matters is that you have a means to tune in with inner guidance and live in greater alignment with your deepest calling. Conscious, connected breathing techniques keep us in the present where we can access the doorway to our intuitive awareness, the part of us that is fully in tune with the natural flow of our truth.

A Powerful Breathing Technique to Facilitate Transitions

The technique for tuning in to inner direction in times of transition is profound in its simplicity. Anytime you desire to resonate more with your guiding truth, follow these steps:

1. Find a quiet place where you can sit undisturbed. Sit upright with your spine straight yet comfortable.
2. Clearly define in your mind (writing often helps), the two or more options with which you are struggling.
3. Take one of the options in your mind and begin to breathe as you think about it.
4. At the same time, begin to breathe in a rhythmic, connected fashion. Inhale smoothly, relax the exhale, and keep the breath connected. In other words, keep a continuous flow as if your breath were like an ocean wave rising and falling with each inhalation and exhalation. It is important not to pause, but to keep the breath connected, and flowing at a slightly accelerated rate, as if you were walking to get some exercise.
5. With the option still in your consciousness, concentrate your awareness of your heart.
6. Notice without judgment what feelings naturally arise. Make note of the quality of your breathing as you dwell on this option.
7. Then take the other option(s) and repeat the same steps, noting the feelings that naturally arise and the ease or difficulty that occurs in

your breathing pattern. For example, are your feelings joyful or apprehensive? Does your breath flow smoothly or is there some difficulty in the process?

As you allow the different options to resonate with or against your authentic energy, it will become apparent which course of action is most compelling. Trust yourself and take it. You will never regret it.

When your journey brings you to an important fork in the road of your life and you have a difficult decision to make – be it personal, romantic, or business – take a few moments to practice this exercise. Tune out the voices of "shoulds," "cants," and expectations of others by tuning in to the deep, inner awareness that peacefully and playfully guides your life in the direction of greatest fulfillment. The results will be different for everyone, so only you can truly know for yourself. This kind of conviction may be daunting, but it is very liberating.

A Life in Alignment with Dharma

Much has happened since the day I spoke with my counselor and my whole life shifted. My decision to leave monastic life has led me on the journey to become a public speaker, wellness practitioner, spiritual leader, and conscious entrepreneur, specializing in life transformation. Yet it is far from an easy lifestyle. On an almost daily basis I am reminded to take personal responsibility for my happiness and face my fear by trusting my intuition. It is important to note that facing fears doesn't mean they simply vanish because you are facing them; in fact, at times it seems like the fear is intensified. Yet I have not regretted my decision for a single minute. When needed, I tune back into the original feelings of my own inner confirmation, accessible through my transformational breathing practices. **There is no substitute for living in alignment with your truth**. If you do not, it will simply not feel good. If you want to experience success in the form of lasting happiness, this alignment is required.

As we continue this journey on the ever-morphing landscape of experience, it becomes apparent that the only constant is change. In order to more successfully manage the changes and transitions in your life, tap into your inspiration by tuning in to your breath. You will not only weather the turbulence of your own transitions more gracefully, but you will also become a vitally important player in assisting the world to navigate through the perpetual waves of change. This is perfect dharma – expressing your individual truth in alignment with universal truth. Live it. Breathe it.

R. CHRISTIAN MINSON is a former monastic, Certified Breathwork Facilitator, and conscious entrepreneur. Through his company, Breathflow Wellness, Christian teaches the application of spiritual principles and breathing techniques to achieve modern-world success and happiness. As the "monk on the street," he has delivered his message to churches, universities, and yoga centers around the country and abroad, as well as contributing to Vision Magazine. For FREE breathing technique downloads and more information, visit his website www.BreathFlow.com.

CHAPTER TWENTY FOUR

Life's Beautiful Blessings
in Disguise

IRIS ROSENFELD, DC

"Life isn't about surviving the storm, it's about dancing in the rain."

— AUTHOR UNKNOWN

"She may not live through the night, and if she does, be prepared. She certainly won't be a ballerina and you may need to institutionalize her."

These were the gut-wrenching, emotionally paralyzing words my husband and I heard from the doctors after giving birth to our premature daughter, Lara, on Christmas Day, 1986. Only three days prior, my water broke, I was admitted to the hospital and then told, "You will be bedridden until you deliver." We were terrified and my entire body starting shivering and shaking as I was in a state of shock. Could this really be happening? My due date wasn't until the middle of March.

After birth, our baby girl was put on every life support apparatus imaginable. When I was able to visit the tiny, wrinkled-looking baby the following day, wires and tubes were attached to most of her body. I found one spot on her hand to touch. In a soft, nurturing voice I said, "This is

Mommy… I'm here… and you are growing stronger and stronger." At that moment, even with a tube protruding from her mouth, she smiled at me and I knew deep down in my soul she was going to be okay.

For the next two months she was in and out of two hospital intensive care units. We were on a roller coaster ride of emotions, dealing with decisions about surgical procedures and medical interventions. So many thoughts were racing through my head: "Do I have the strength, courage, and fortitude to deal with all of this? Could this really be happening, or was it just a bad dream? How will I be able to handle repayment of my student loans, business loans for my newly-established chiropractic practice, and car loan payments? Will our marriage of less than a year survive?"

On one hand, we felt so grateful to gaze into Lara's bright brown eyes, treasure the laughs, exhilarate in her warm and engaging smile, and delight in her joy and beauty. However, she was unable to turn over, crawl or move like other babies her age. At two years old she was officially diagnosed with cerebral palsy – specifically spastic diplegia (two extremities are spastic). At that moment I became a victim, feeling sorry for myself and unable to stop the tears from pouring down my face. As I looked at this sweet, innocent, precious gift, I could do nothing but feel enveloped in sadness for her as well as for me.

After a week of being in deep sorrow, feeling overwhelmed by my painful circumstances, my body emotionally and physically wounded, I made a life-changing decision. I decided I would take action in the face of fear, devoting myself to doing whatever it took to provide the opportunities for our baby girl to meet her fullest potential, whatever that might look like, despite my self-doubts, fear of the unknowns, and sense of limitations.

As the years progressed, I had to give up **all my initial preconceptions and expectations of what I thought it would "be like and look like" to raise our child.** I was performing a juggling act between the medical, social, and educational needs of our daughter, my growing chiropractic practice, our home and our marriage. My daily commitments and passionate resilience in regard to every personal and professional detail filled my life. I have been blessed to be in a healing profession that gives me the opportunity to make a difference to those I touch structurally, nutritionally and emotionally. Immersed in deep satisfaction in creating abundant miracles by serving and educating others regularly, I continue to eliminate the interferences that lead to dysfunction, poor health, pain, and disease. This inspired path enabled me to move beyond my personal crises.

At about seven years old, our inquisitive and charming daughter was disturbed by the way her peers, and even adults, stared at her. In my opinion, she resembled Cleopatra, with her curly brown hair flowing halfway down her back, olive complexion, and petite stature. However, her spastic legs warranted the use of bilateral foot orthotics and she needed the assistance of a walker or wheelchair for ambulation. She learned by speaking with a child psychologist friend of ours, even at this very young age, that although she couldn't change her body image from the outside, she could let her soul shine by just saying "Hi" and smiling when others stared at her.

Through the years we learned creativity, resiliency, and consistently thinking outside the box as we were vigilant about exploring life's fullest opportunities. We paved the way for others in the community through being role models for the disabled, and created awareness about access-challenged environments. Through the loving support of my husband, our family, and our spiritual community, we persevered through two additional major surgeries with hope, faith, and determination.

During the past four years, our uniquely gifted daughter has been attending the University of Berkeley, 400 miles from home, focusing on her committed dreams of being a film/television writer and empowering the disabled community. Although she was struck by a car while crossing the street on the college campus a few years ago and became pessimistic, questioning her chosen path, she was able to conquer her uncertainties and overwhelming fears and choose to be the champion in her life. Lara continues to show courage, embrace the power within herself, thrive in the face of life's extreme traumas, and inspire others through her intuitive gifts and transforming inner wisdom.

Looking back at the past 23 years, I see how my mindset of balance, integrity, and commitment was and continues to be engrained in my DNA both personally and professionally. Knowing that since I was very young my compassion for others was my sacred gift, I continue to create a safe and nurturing home and work environment for optimal healing to occur. As a teenager and young adult, I observed unethical choices being made by so-called respectable adults, and knew integrity would be a core value at the forefront of my life's journey.

How do I stay focused in spite of every challenging circumstance thrown in my path? Ultimately, I decide to be attentive to my purpose and my "why," despite the most difficult situations. For example, in my first year of my own practice in 1985, all my medical equipment was stolen from the doctor I was sharing an office with. Rather than giving in to despair, I recognized it as an opportunity to change direction. With my thirst for learning and expanding spiritually, I continued to pursue coursework in total wellness. I saw that the traditional chiropractic model of healing did not accomplish my health vision for my patients, so I regularly expanded my medical expertise. At times, I get frustrated with how the insurance companies attempt to mold our health decisions. I fundamentally know I cannot live in that place of frustration, as that would steal my healing energy for others. Therefore, I ask myself, "Has there ever been a time in my life when I have had no problems?" Probably not, so I focus my life on creating empowerment. I draw my strength against insurmountable odds by relying on past successes.

There are a number of key steps that continue to aid me throughout my life's adventures in obtaining my balance in conscious living. I've learned that life will never be perfect, so I strive to do my best. My life has been built upon my own unique gifts and talents, which I'm passionate about and which wake me up every morning. Therefore, tasks that I consider uninteresting and/or technologically challenging are delegated to a support team of enthusiastic experts.

Letting go of "figuring it all out" or "knowing it all," sometimes to my detriment, has been of great benefit on my profound journey. Routinely, I recreate a set of realistic expectations for myself and those around me. Being an inspiration to others and assisting them with their goals has supported me during the stormy roadblocks and obstacles.

I use my birthday each year to not only celebrate, but also to contemplate my achievements from the prior year, and what I would like to create before my next birthday in regard to my health, relationships, finances, career, dreams, etc. Additionally, I use this time to give someone else a gift.

When I put my head down on my pillow each night to go to sleep, I stay connected to the power of my thoughts by acknowledging any failures of the day and replaying the victories. I get rid of any ANTS – **A**utomatic **N**egative **T**houghts – that may steal my dreams. I quiet my mind through deep-breathing exercises and visual imagery.

I now face any obstacles that come into my path as an entrepreneur with an open heart, thanks to lessons learned through my daughter. I sincerely believe that many of life's adversities turn out to be blessings in disguise.

IRIS ROSENFELD, DC, a published author, has been awarded Woman of the Year. She founded her Chiropractic Wellness Center in 1985. Her services are masterfully tailored to meet one's needs structurally, nutritionally and emotionally through eliminating the interferences that lead to dysfunction, pain, and disease. To learn more about upcoming in-office and community enlightening workshops, receive free instructive newsletters and create miraculous breakthroughs in abundant longevity, health and vitality, go to www.DrIris.com.

CHAPTER TWENTY FIVE

How My Soul Took Me Around the World and Back Again

PREM DANA TAKADA
B.B.Sc. (HONS.), M. PSYCH. (CLIN.)

POONA, INDIA: IMMERSE YOURSELF. TOTALLY.

I never imagined that one day I would find myself in lush southern India, dressed in a long maroon robe, dancing and singing in a Buddha field. I had yet to appreciate the full implications of what following the calling of my soul meant, but already it had led me half way around the world to the UK and had now planted me firmly in the soil of meditation in ancient India. I had somewhere along my path ignited a desire to radically reform my life. I knew I could not do it alone and that I had to immerse myself in an atmosphere of a totally new way of living, based on a passion for transforming blocks and transcending the shackles of conditioning.

Yes, there was a man involved. We met and worked in the Mystery School where we studied the exploration of the alchemical sciences. He was dark, exotic, and handsome. I was compelled to follow this new destiny which would take me on yet another journey – this time to Japan. But there were some other lessons first.

MELBOURNE, AUSTRALIA: DON'T HESITATE. GO!

During my childhood and young adulthood, no-one inquired, "What lies in your heart? What is your innermost heart's desire?" let alone tell me that if I followed it I was destined for success. Yet somehow I was one of the lucky ones. In 1979, at the tender age of 17, I was enrolled in first year psychology at a Melbourne university. The study of this subject I would, in fact, never leave, and I continued to explore it in all its permutations and combinations over three decades.

Hindsight is a funny thing. All I can say is whenever the next step revealed itself, I took it – almost without thinking – with a blind faith that no one else seemed to believe in but me.

I remember being told in that huge auditorium filled with fresh, eager, first year students, to give up any dreams of becoming a clinical psychologist since there were so few positions available for that profession. (As I recall there were only eight in the cohort who succeeded.) Crush. Stomp. Yet, when it was time, I prepared myself and was ready.

Now, where did this faith to follow my soul's meanderings come from? I have suffered, and continue in some ways to suffer, from self-esteem issues, fear issues, and nagging doubt along with most people. All I can say is that when I hear the call I listen and I go. It's that simple. The knack was always to get out of my own way so I could listen and then to keep going! One day I was guided to leave Australia and seek my fortune abroad. As I said goodbye to my family at the airport two days after my 30th birthday, they had no idea that I would be gone for over 16 years.

LONDON, UK: UNDERSTAND LOVE – YOUR ESSENCE.

My name, Prem Dana, is a meditation name. It means "the act of giving love." In 1991 I worked for National Health in West London as a principal psychologist. I was a caring, considerate person and am sure that my friends, clients, and work colleagues admired and liked me. Yet inside I still spent most of my energy trying to get love. London, city of materialism and capitalism, was funnily enough where I began to learn the lesson of love. In business or relationships, we need always to come from a sense of already being full, of already experiencing the essential truth that we are deeply and inherently loved. If not, we come from a place of need and lack that burdens our relationship with our partner and interferes with our business. It is only after already having esteem and love deep within us that we can then express, share, and give of ourselves in these relationships. Understanding this is paramount. I use my meditation name in my daily working life to remind me of this truth.

Florida, USA: Overcome Fear. A Reason Why.

I did it! It was 2002 and I offered a presentation at what was at that time the biggest psychotherapy conference in the U.S. My topic was alchemical psychotherapy and hypnotherapy – a six-step process for transforming problems through a combination of heart meditations and Jungian polarization of opposites. However, before the event, I was terrified. Completely. In fact, I was sure I would be ruthlessly criticized (my #1 paralyzing fear) by the person who had selected me to present, Dr. Jeffrey Zeig. I didn't understand why he selected me, and his confidence didn't stop my paranoia. Nor did the fact that I had already presented this material successfully across Asia.

How to get out of my fear? Only one method worked. I thought long and hard about the reason why I wanted to make the presentation. I had been studying with the world masters in transformational work for years and had uniquely blended these teachings while adding my own essence to them. **I knew I was meant to share this.** My new goal: If just one person was touched and transformed by my offering, that was success. This thought immediately calmed and soothed me, putting the focus squarely where it belonged – on those that I am in the service of. Overcoming fear through really knowing why has been crucial to my being of service and transforming many thousands of people's lives.

TOKYO, JAPAN: CO-CREATE MIRACLES.

I can honesty say I am an accidental entrepreneur. I took another jump into my soul in 1995 when I went to Japan. I had to create my own business as there were no jobs! So I launched what was to be a very successful private enterprise. I have always been blessed with perfect timing and the time was ripe for my services. It is a very satisfying feeling creating something from a blank tablet – to be paid for what I alone was offering, not hiding behind a company or department. It initially left me feeling exposed, bare, and vulnerable, but the rewards far outweighed the initial fears. **I just knew I had to do it.**

I put a three months' deposit down for rent on a consulting office at exorbitant Tokyo prices. I arranged to stay part-time in my salaried position to help pay for it all, doing work that I did not love, but I went to work one day and I was no longer on the roster! I walked out and away from anyone having power over me ever again, ignoring thinly-veiled threats involving immigration and taxes.

The very next week, an interview I had done appeared in The Japan Times, the national English newspaper. My phone did not stop ringing. The universe was conspiring for my success and doors opened as if by magic. When I heed my "soul purpose," I live in a world where miracles unfold every day. Life becomes guided, empowered, and easy.

BYRON BAY, AUSTRALIA: FIND HOME

Rocks do talk. I was sitting on a rock on the most easterly point of Australia at Byron Bay, along a path that climbs up to a magnificent lighthouse at its peak, when I heard a voice say: "This is your home now. Great choice!" I thought, since I believe this to be one of the most beautiful places on Planet Earth. Though it took me a few years and several major obstacles to make it my permanent home, it was this place that welcomed me with open arms and heart upon my return for the next level of the unfolding of my soul's journey. This time I would share my vast knowledge and experience in cutting-edge modern psychology, and change technologies alongside ancient spiritual tools and wisdom that I have gathered from so many world masters in all corners of the world. I would inspire and teach others how to find their soul and utilize its power as a catalyst for transforming lives. To express your soul wholeheartedly in the world is everyone's divine birthright. It's true. When the inner home has been found, the outer home appears.

As I sit here writing this, it seems almost impossible to communicate what it feels like to know in my heart that if you learn how to listen and follow your own soul's blueprint for you, your life tomorrow will no longer resemble the one you have today. My studio office is surrounded by lush tropical gardens. My Abyssinian cat sleeks through the door and nestles himself down on my leather consulting chair. I hear my husband – yes, the same guy from the Indian story – playing with our son, laughing and squealing. And no, long robes are not compulsory, though feel free to wear them if you wish!

How to Transform Your Life at the Speed of Soul:

1. **Remember** who you really are.
2. **Immerse** yourself in communities of like-minded souls.
3. **Go fearlessly** – transform old energies and blocks.
4. Enjoy manifesting **miracles.**
5. **Come home.**

PREM DANA TAKADA, B.B.Sc. (Hons) M.Psych. (Clin.) is founder and creator of Byron Psychology, "Soul Speed Transformation," and "Soul Purpose 2 Market" products and services. She has led individuals, couples, and group processes and trainings in Australia, Asia, Europe and the U.S., successfully transforming thousands of people's lives, relationships, and work places from pain and suffering to joy and freedom. Go to www.SoulSpeedTransformation.com now and receive a FREE gift from the heart for your speed transformation.

CHAPTER TWENTY SIX

Asian Awakening

LINDA TAYLOR

When they opened the door to show me into my new "apartment" I was literally speechless, as in, "You've got to be kidding, right?" It was only one room. One wall was all window, one wall was all mirror, and it was located above a bar and restaurant which had this huge neon sign – on the other side of the window which had no curtains! This was to be my living quarters for the next year while I taught English at an elementary school in South Korea.

The school had already decided that I would also teach classes at a sister school which was even farther out into the countryside than I already was. The very small village where I now lived had no other English-speaking people, and I was looked at as an oddity when I went to the bank or walked to the store with my backpack so that I wouldn't have to buy and tote plastic bags of groceries back to my very tiny apartment. There were no restaurants where I could order food, as I didn't read Korean at the time, plus I am allergic to shellfish and pork, staples of their diet. I had never had to use a bus, and again, couldn't read the signs to know where it was going, so one of the other teachers came to pick me up every morning.

At least I was shown how to use a bank card, and if I could see numbers, I could render the correct amount of Korean won when I did purchase anything.

Yes, the culture shock lasted almost six months! However, eventually I did find my way around and adapted to the lifestyle of an expat, even learning how to take the bus into Seoul (over an hour away), and use the subway to get around in a city of eleven million people! It was the beginning of the journey to find the real me.

Over the next couple of years I came to realize quite a bit about myself. I became aware of the incredible amount of fear that possessed me, even though I used to tell people that having survived raising two teenaged sons, nothing could scare me. The truth is I was afraid to live, to know who I really was, to experience life and live full-out! There were plenty of differences in my life now as far as living arrangements, financial security, relationships with co-workers, and after work activities. Certainly the one room apartment was much different than the five-bedroom, four-bath house in a nice area of a major city in Texas where I lived when I was married.

The most startling realization came when I observed how much was similar in what I was attracting into my life. The job that was supposed to be exciting became a drudge to go to daily. The fear about not having enough money to survive and support myself into retirement constantly sat at the back of my mind. The new relationships that I formed were not as supportive and nurturing as I had imagined.

The transportation issue was challenging, if not daunting, being located in the middle of the peninsula and not being brave enough to go exploring for fear of getting lost. So many people thought I was brave because I had gotten rid of everything to set out on this new adventure, not knowing much of anything about the country of South Korea. Little did they know, or me for that matter, how uncourageous I really felt!

At one point, with pen and paper, I began to write down all that was similar from before and what was showing up at present, which was mostly what I **didn't want** and what I **didn't like**! This provided me with a picture of what I was actually attracting into my life. By the choices I was making, I realized that I was recreating the same scenario. Now **that** was surprising! I had recently begun a study of the Law of Attraction and became entranced by the possibilities of creating one's own reality. Thinking back to the feelings that I had when making each of those choices, I began to see a pattern emerging. This was a most helpful step in becoming aware of how unwise some of those decisions truly were, and in becoming aware of the multiple OTHER choices that had been available to me.

I continued to read books and articles about personal development and natural laws, listen to audios of various self-help gurus and search for answers as I explored my own consciousness by asking questions of myself. How could I turn this around and actually attract and live the life of my dreams? I continued to search all topics related to the Law of Attraction and hired a coach who gently guided me to the realization of my innate power and the gift within my being. Then I began writing and clarifying what I did want in all areas of my life.

I wrote, clarified, and rewrote, imagining the feeling of actually experiencing what I had written… and then it happened. Things began to show up that I had described in my writing, such as the exact apartment that I imagined, a better car to drive, and a job near the area that I preferred to live. Gradually the process began and then continued to show up, much like a motor which has stalled and then begins to come back to life slowly, by generating movement until it picks up speed.

Here is what I learned about life and what to remember when going through difficult circumstances: The awareness of the need for change starts with our stories, and everyone has them. By rehearsing them, that is, telling them over and over again, they become embedded as beliefs – as the truth to us, and all of these stories have emotions attached to them, mostly negative. By repeating past events, they become rooted. Some are worth remembering time and time again, like the birth of one's first child, or accolades that were awarded for a job or performance well done. Others, not so positive, take one's mind back to places best released and not revisited. Remaining in the past allows us to assume the position of victimhood, which should be avoided at all costs.

Another learning point was that all decisions have consequences, which have feelings attached and energy that is put into those feelings. The baggage of emotional energy, even though I had changed my geographic location, continued to affect what was still being attracted into my life. It was when I began to understand myself and accept who I was, that I was able to begin the process of releasing the past. The energy, both positive and negative, propels and sustains the position so that one can either continue to feel bad, or choose to feel good. It is through energy that we control our life by our choices.

Life is lived in the present. While we remember the past or hope for the future, we have to live the here and now. The choices we make today do affect the future. The more understanding we have about ourselves in the present, the more we are free of the energy which binds us to the past. Being aware and observing what you are thinking and how you are reacting is a message and a lesson for us. Learning the lessons given and accepting the message, we are then empowered to move ahead into our full potential.

My experience has been both an emotional and a physical journey – a passage of time that has led me to a deeper understanding of myself and the world around me – one in which ultimately I created and attracted the events, the people, the circumstances and the situations which showed up. When I look at who I am now and how far I have moved, I realize that my present decisions, actions, and choices actually create my next moments, tomorrows, and my future.

Always remember that there is a time factor involved, which is the duration of the process. Realize that you didn't get to the point of wanting change as quickly as you want out of the uncomfortable or difficult situation, because that takes a process of time.

Some suggestions if you find yourself in need of a makeover:

1. Write out in detail, with specific clarity, what you DO want. Keep revising and adding to this until it feels right and makes your heart smile.
2. Listen to motivational speakers, audios, videos – anything that lifts your emotions will put you in a place to attract better experiences now and in the future. Seriously consider finding a coach to work with.
3. Allow the past to be there! Consider it a learning phase, accept the lesson, and let go of anything negative. This will provide you with the freedom to embrace peace, joy, and wonder in your present and in your future!

LINDA TAYLOR is a certified coach, a teacher, and a success mentor. She is the first Higher-Consciousness Attraction Coach graduate from Law of Attraction Training Center, as well as from The Energy Coach Institute. An international speaker and author currently living in South Korea, she leads and facilitates a monthly gathering about Law of Attraction. She can be reached by visiting her website at: www.ReInventYourLifeCoaching.com.

CHAPTER TWENTY SEVEN

Intergenerational Business: A Harmonious Integration of Life and Work

LIZ ZED

"I'll let you be in my dream if I can be in yours." Bob Dylan said that. He's a cocky wordsmith, a "humdinger folksinger." To me, they sound like words out of the mouth of a business owner, as a challenge to a target market.

Today, as an impassioned psychologist answering my calling as a business coach, Dylan's words describe how I experience what we might call a privileged exchange between business owners and their clients and customers. It's the idea of clients letting me "be in their dream," as I grant them access to "be in my dream." It's a joyous dance – being in one another's dreams – moving businesses toward being sustainable and long-lived.

I didn't always think like this. Once upon a time, a long time ago and back in the day, my career was high-stress child protection. I acquired a jaded view, apprehending serious abusers of children.

Even further back in time, I had been an avidly-committed, trail-blazing researcher of first-time fathers. Optimistic hypothesizing as a researcher morphed into disillusionment as a child protector. What good was I doing?

So, I quit that government job, setting out with an intention to shift my jaded view. The goal was transformation to a more hopeful perspective, dedicating myself to full-time child rearing in a move from the megalopolis to a sandy beach at the edge of nowhere.

You can imagine those days: earth-mothering was neither trail-blazing nor chic. The unexpected move alienated colleagues who did not comprehend my aim. That aim was to test some of what developmental psychology would have us believe against some different principles, based on observations of child rearing in a primitive tribal culture. And more!

Today, as a "funmeister" business and lifestyle-design coach, it's a bird's-eye view I take, looking as if from above at the path taken to get here. As a trail-blazing researcher of new fathers, feminist, social psychology academic, and urban working mother, role-modeling the outrageously successful woman who does it all, I came to be viewed by peers as the quintessential "sell-out" of working mothers everywhere. I sadly shook my head, packed, and moved to the beach beside the rain forest.

What did I find there? Idyllic abundance; play and hard work; an off-the-grid, back-to-the-land lifestyle with hand-tooled home-building, gardening, and raising children – it was all there. For a while it was bliss! That is, until the money ran out. But without income and sustainability, bliss doesn't last. One world disintegrates. A new one forms.

Craving to share with everyone the delight and deluxity of my gigantic, sandbox paradise led to a wonderfully synchronistic experience and an adventure in surf-shop proprietorship and family business. While asking myself, "Why wouldn't everybody want to have this much fun? How can I make this edge-of-the-ocean-waves adventure/lifestyle sustainable?" Divine intelligence graciously appeared and answered. A new era "surf mama"/"surfing the shore since '84" was born. This single-parent adventurer/founder/president birthed a surf business into being.

In '84, I didn't yet have the requisite necessities for dynamic and great success in business. These – systems skills, organizational skills, discipline, productivity, time management, money management, team leadership – had to be cultivated over time as did food from our garden. Learning as I went, "business owner" became just another facet of the parent role. How lucky the children were to acquire these with me. A sustainable, intergenerational business is an adventure in child rearing – bigger than big!

Fraught with obstacles and difficulties, tenacity and perseverance **are** required! Looking back, I cringe a little at the hardship of starting a business. Cultivating perseverance can start with your asking yourself why you want to be a business owner. It's an essential question. A compelling answer will help keep you "keeping on" rather than your being one of the "tough" who get going "when the going gets tough."

Have you heard that before achieving great success, the encountering of great resistance is common? An ability to see obstacles as opportunities is helpful, and even more so when acquired in childhood. Children fortunate enough to be raised amid a growing, family business experience enough obstacles to understand the advantage and necessity of turning them into opportunities.

Opportunity abounds for a founder to lead by example. In my case, with a family to lead and to support financially, I wanted to "be" and teach financial leadership to my children. Creating and building this business – in exactly the way I envisioned it from its inception – was a wonderful framework for living my most important values! Family members shared creative expression and bountiful learning with fun and plenty of satisfaction.

These aren't enough, though. Ultimately, to stay in business you must make money. If you're not making money, you just have a hobby. I'm reminded that "Money is liquid creativity." I've heard spiritual counselor and author, Sonia Choquette, say this about money. Creativity abounds growing a family business!

Inside the ultimate, creative playground of a family business, making money is fun! Being able to live and work in close proximity gave me and my two young children fun and creativity in spades. Not every family wants to work where they live, though.

I believe destiny intervened in our "live:work" decision. Living a conscious and intentional lifestyle with the ability to attend to the whispers of wisdom and guidance is a wonderful asset. My initial business plan didn't include business and home together. Guidance appeared that the originally-chosen location in the village's commercial hub wasn't going to work. It wasn't difficult to take notice and act on this guidance when it appeared. "Lifestyle design" was already important. Often though, our conscious and other-than-conscious selves are not in alignment! Then it can be difficult to hear guidance or to take the right actions, and we may face more difficult dilemmas and decisions.

Like a first time parent, being a first time business owner brings with it a need for implementation of new systems. How often have you heard new parents express shock at how much time it suddenly takes just to get ready to go somewhere? There's a raft of new things in the routine that were not there before Baby. The newly-harried householder busily figuring out all the things they need to remember is checking to make sure there isn't something important they might be leaving behind. Then there's another diaper change, or another feeding, or any number of other interruptions. An entirely new system is needed just to get out the door!

A new business is like that all the time. Considering that systems can be critical to success, all kinds of helpful systems can be borrowed from other entrepreneurs. But often starting solo means isolation and "lone-rangering," and we get stuck re-inventing the wheel! A new venture can adopt systems, but many will require substantial alteration to work in a new environment. Invented on the fly, others exemplify the creative adventure of business building! Children are good systems designers. Ever the fabulous creators and innovators, children love contributing.

Kids learn fast. They delight in learning by doing and by teaching others. Their inventiveness is startling! If children find a challenge that impacts them in some way, watch them give it their all trying to create a functional solution. They are also great at creating practical and imaginative ways to design new products.

Kids inspire drive in their business-owner parents to increase disposable income for the kind of experiences, adventures, and education parents want to expose their kids to, or share with them. Increased family time now required to play and learn together stimulates team-building, which improves effectiveness. It helps decrease isolation and lone ranger ways of trying to do things, accomplishing little.

Business-owner parents have the perfect opportunity to impart money management skills, while teaching their kids how to manage earnings. Creative investing games make this part of an ongoing, fun adventure, and provide the beginnings of a financial, foundational, asset building-block for them.

Bookkeeping is an imperative not to be forgotten! Hand this off later. In the beginning, know your financial recordkeeping. Teach, delegate, and teach how to delegate. Teaching children how to keep the books is ideal hands-on business fundamentals training. Knowing how to manage money – theirs and other's – will assist their success as adult entrepreneurs after they catch the entrepreneurial bug from their business-owner mom or dad.

Intergenerational business ownership provides unlimited opportunity to create great employer and team-builder skills. What you model for your children becomes the foundation of how they lead, partner, and follow others. Model for them an ability to communicate, be compassionate and fair-minded, and assist others to be empowered. Teach them how to show up as business-owner parents of the future!

Enjoy a phenomenal family adventure owning an intergenerational business. The experience will impart to your children a deep understanding of these words of Flavia Weedn: "If one dream should fall and break into a thousand pieces, never be afraid to pick one of those pieces up and begin again." It's an opportunity to hone a great capacity for resilience.

Never straying far from joy, *DR. LIZ ZED* is true to her unique vision of entrepreneurial success and designed lifestyle. Her visioning strategies for action and success are perfected methods and techniques culled from decades of experience and many masters of diverse disciplines across the globe. She has assisted thousands of students and clients from wayward youth to elders of the C-suite to change their game. For business coaching and raising conscious entrepreneurs, you can contact her at Liz@VividVisionCoaching.com.

PART THREE

Succeed

CHAPTER TWENTY EIGHT

Align, Contract, Collapse: A Story of Death and Rebirth

MARCIA AVALON

Night is the worst time. I dread going to bed. I can manage the fear during the day. Breathe. Meditate. Strategize.

But fear rules at night, turning my bedroom into a torture chamber. I am trapped in a dungeon where the cement walls contract closer each day, leaving me less air to breathe, less room to move – squeezing me to death. Fear controls every part of my body. It wakes me often to witness my anguish.

"How can this be happening to me?" I ask over and over. I get no response.

I re-live how I got into this prison of debt that will swallow my home, my business, my income, my savings, my daughter's home, her business, and her income. I cringe in shame at making bad decisions and in guilt over losing my retirement money.

Knowing that many people have been in this situation is no comfort. I am a prisoner in solitary confinement.

CREATION

My story, like most entrepreneurs' stories, begins with determination to move forward into a better life. As a disillusioned management consultant whose role is to align organizations with vague and futile corporate strategies, I am seeking more autonomy, more fulfillment, and more real value.

"Do what you love and the money will follow," is a great business plan, I thought.

Starting at age 20, I remodeled and redesigned every house I owned and sold each of them quickly to delighted new owners. "I can turn my gift into a fun and fulfilling family business," I thought.

It is a wonderful alignment of our individual gifts and goals. My daughter, Marisa, shares my passion and talent for transforming personal living space. Her husband Eric is a "do-it-the-right-way" master carpenter and determined problem-solver. Marisa is good with numbers. I am a business strategist and designer. All of us want work-from-home freedom, self-expression, and self-generated income. They will learn to run the operation and later manage it without me while I enjoy a world-traveling retirement.

Our unique niche in the market is clear: vintage homes in great neighborhoods. Captivated by the distinctive charms of old houses, we feel a calling to restore their souls and deliver them to new caretakers who will write a new chapter in their history. "Terrific Transformations, LLC" will benefit families, neighborhoods, and local communities.

"Wow! We can so do this," we agree.

Marisa flees her corporate cubicle with her hair on fire and moves her family from San Francisco to Portland, Oregon. Working together as a family is a dream about to come true. We begin our venture with inspiration, good intentions, and exuberant high energy.

EXPANSION

Things are going well in our labor-of-love business. It is indeed our vehicle for self-expression – fueled by values, vision, talent, integrity, energy, and hard work.

Our transformed homes are works of art and comfort. Marisa and I stage them to highlight their vintage beauty and family livability. Eric is proud to guarantee the solid quality of workmanship in each house. Buyers fall in love. Our gorgeous homes sell quickly for top dollar. Other investors call to learn what we do.

Stretching mentally, physically, and financially, we confidently (with fingers crossed), expand into bigger homes, more properties, bigger crews, and more professional advisors. The need for money becomes more urgent. So does the push to finish projects quickly. Our stress levels escalate.

CONTRACTION

We feel the economic storm coming. I make plans to sell all our properties before the winds and waves of a rapidly contracting market engulf us, but we are duty-bound to complete work we have started. I push Eric and the crews to work faster. I put every cent I have towards finishing on time.

I understand why we are vulnerable. Our business model holds the seeds of disaster. Long project cycles and unforeseen costs consume more and more cash and time. We are entangled in more and more bank and credit card loans.

I understand why the market is contracting. The old model, dependent on rapid increase of both property values and mass credit, has become unworkable. While I fully expect the financial hurricane to come, I pray that we can avoid a fatal impact. I am trying desperately to evacuate, but the escape routes are closed. There is no choice but to stay and take the hit. And hope for a miracle.

The confusion, agitation, and stress of acknowledging the inevitable, while desperately trying to hang on, own my every moment. My self-torture begins.

As the markets in other areas of the country collapse, my stress turns to absolute terror.

DESTRUCTION AND COLLAPSE

The miracle I've been praying for doesn't happen. We don't escape. We are hit.

Our business dies, erasing everything we created, leaving us with nothing but the inescapable: no income, foreclosure, moving, collection agents, bankruptcy, guilt, and shame.

The whole economy teeters on collapse. We are only one of the millions of fatalities. We are part of the discarded debris. The collapse dumps us into the vague, uncertain seas of the new economy.

But to my astonishment, I sleep through the nights. My mind is quiet. My body is still. Like water after a storm, my fear subsides. My terror evaporates.

The collapse is the miracle! It is the healer – the provider of the solution.

We have contracted back to zero. Yet, strangely, zero turns out to be a wonderful number. Certainly better than the negative numbers we have been anguishing over. Vastly better than trying to stop the wave from crashing in on us.

The only thing I can control is how I see my situation and how I choose to respond.

REFLECTION

I allow myself lots of quiet time to meditate on my situation. I open my mind and heart to see clearly. I not only accept our destruction, I bless and embrace it. I am full of gratitude. I begin to see the small miracles appearing in my life which keep us afloat. They keep us safe and sane.

I am grateful for being kicked into the future, into a new life and a fresh start. I am a fatality, but not a victim.

Here are the insights from my reflection:

1. Evolution is a natural, ongoing process of continual creation and destruction.

I forgot I knew that. I got caught up in the lie that progress can go on forever in a straight line. That humans can be in complete control. That we can have only creation without destruction.

Sometimes I catch myself waiting for things to "get back to normal," but I know that we are not going back to the old economy. We can only dance with the evolving economy as it unfolds – an intuitive dance of influence and acceptance, acceptance and influence.

How do you experience the cycle of creation and destruction?

2. It is time for new definitions of "value."

I consciously designed Terrific Transformations to deliver several kinds of value, but it would not be enough in the new economy. My new vision has to be bigger.

Businesses can create many kinds and levels of value. Financial value is important, but not sufficient. Personal expression and fulfillment are essential, but not adequate.

Our businesses, large and small, must offer value to our customers, prospects, market, industry, partners, competitors, communities, and planet. Co-created value means greater mutual benefit.

What new definitions of value do you see?

3. On my own, I do not know what I do not know.

In hindsight I would change many of my business decisions. I can see where I was blind, wrong, or stubborn. There are people and projects I would not have gotten involved with had I known the impact.

There were so many things I didn't know – and didn't know that I didn't know. They led to fatal and near-fatal mistakes, not only during the creation and expansion of the business, but also in the collapse, recovery, and start up. I could have discovered my blind spots by asking more questions and having conversations with others who did know.

When have you not known something and didn't know that you didn't know? What were the results?

REGENERATION AND REBIRTH

I am building my new business, Ask Real Experts, on these insights. It requires a higher consciousness and a big vision of greater contribution. It is designed to:

1. Dance – be able to lead or follow as needed in any situation. The principles of evolution are at its core.

2. Provide value to everyone it touches and seek out multiple opportunities for co-creation and mutual benefit.

3. Create conversations among the experts who have the challenges and the subject experts who have solutions.

What insights have you gleaned from your experiences? What do they lead you to create?

MARCIA AVALON, Ph.D., founder of Ask Real Experts, brings experts in a wide range of topics to teach service professionals, entrepreneurs, and start-ups how to avoid making fatal and near-fatal mistakes, and to build solid, comprehensive value instead. Value-focused owners engender confidence, fulfillment, and financial success for themselves, their market, customers, staff, business, community, and industry. Go to www.AskRealExperts.com to find secrets and solutions to your business challenges. Download *The Business Value Loop* for FREE.

CHAPTER TWENTY NINE

Make the Choice – Now or Never

WILMA J. BROWN

"Either you decide to stay in the shallow end of the pool or you go out in the ocean."

~ CHRISTOPHER REEVE

In 2003, I turned fifty years young. Seeing that age was absolutely a wake-up call that put me and keeps me in a state of gratitude at all times, no matter what.

My work career was beginning to shift and this milestone more than ever put me into "search mode" to find my purpose in life.

I reflected on the fact that my mother passed away at the age of 59, totally unexpectedly, and the thought of that got my attention big time. When she died, I shared that I would never retire from a "job" but would do what I loved until I died.

Being reared by illiterate grandparents who instilled the foundation in me to be the best in all you do, to never judge or think badly about others, and to reach for the stars was phenomenal. If it were left up to Granny, I would have started kindergarten and gone nonstop straight to earning a PhD. It didn't happen that way, but it may happen yet.

Life sent me back to school after being out of that scene for twenty-three years. I had lost my job for the third time in my work career and it was something about that third job loss that led me back to school. This was by far one of the hardest things I had done in my adult life. There were times when I questioned my sanity, but what helped me were words of encouragement from classmates a semester ahead of me. I remember the statement from a high school classmate and friend: "If it were easy, don't you think everyone would have a graduate degree?" I **committed** to the process and graduated two years later.

During graduate school I worked full-time as a trainer. It's funny; I never wanted to teach school and yet I ended up teaching adults, even firefighters.

By 2004. I had worked my way up to training administrator. I began to sense that my skills were being put on the back burner. Management changed, and each time that happened it meant change for the workforce. I am one whose life has made me embrace change as my entire life has been one change after another.

I have been in the workplace most of my adult life in various industries and positions, and I can see and feel the signs when something is not right.

I went along with the agenda at the job and it got to the point where I was training very little. This began to frustrate me and instead of taking it personally, I started focusing on being in business for myself. I did not know how it was going to happen – I just knew it would.

Being a baby boomer, we are the generation that went the extra mile in everything we did, and I became very aware of skills I had that contributed to each position I held. I knew I had a way with people, and the clerical skills I acquired in much younger years stayed with me. I was technical enough to be dangerous, and my customer service skills were above average.

As I faced the fact that my skills were being under-utilized in my current position, I began setting things in motion and investing in myself through workshops, getting on the speaking circuit (which I dearly love at every opportunity I find), being around and networking with people who were doing what I wanted to do and be, making plans, constantly getting outside my comfort zone, and looking ahead.

I have had setbacks too numerous to count, but I never let them stop me. I would get back up and ask, "What is there to learn from this?" I know firsthand how difficult it is to pursue and live your life purpose. It is hard. I often think that things do happen for a reason and it is left up to each of us to test our own inner toughness.

This process went on nearly six years too long, and it was in 2008 that I shifted gears in mind, body, and spirit. I knew that I did not want to start a new "job" at this point in my career or life, which is not to say I could not be hired. I was simply at a place where I had had enough of working for someone else.

I knew things were going downhill for me when I was informed that I would be going to another department doing work that was not in my area of expertise, even though I had the skills to fulfill the position. I approached this work shift as if it were a game I would have to play until I made a move to leave for good.

My family does not understand my desire to live my purpose, but my cousin, Faye, who is with me through thick and thin, can be counted on to lean on and sometimes cry on her shoulder when it seems things are at their worst. I kept mum to my friends about my desire to be in business for myself, for I wanted this process to be between me and God. That way everyone would find out what I was up to at the same time and I would not have to use my energies explaining.

I have had a number of life experiences that taught me that you can not share everything with everyone. People mean well in their own right and yet the bottom line is, it is best to communicate with "like-minds." Not everyone listening to you is with you or for you.

The changes I went through from 2004 to this moment were all what I consider lessons in life. A major event in 2009 was the death of my brother, my only sibling, who lived in California. I had to take care of the entire matter alone, and yet I endured.

I learned things about myself at this time and I realized that I could not move forward until I let go of "stuff" from the past. That meant false beliefs, people who were holding me back, fear of the unknown, and believing I had to do it all by myself. I learned to let go and let my "trusted source" handle it.

At the beginning of 2010, I endured another setback at the workplace that led me to pick up the telephone and call the human resources department to check my status for deferring my retirement. The most amazing thing happened after the conversation when my questions had been answered: I hung up the phone feeling a huge weight had been lifted off my shoulders. It was as if God was saying to me, "Step out Wilma, I will be with you." I knew at this time that I had made the right choice. I had that very same feeling when I decided that I was going to leave my husband.

I did not know how things would work out – I just knew they would. All I knew was that I was leaving, and I never looked back. It meant starting over and yet that was a good thing – a new beginning. The same applies now.

I am certain that by the time this book is published I will be in business for myself as a consultant – training, speaking, facilitating workshops – a published author – doing all the things I love. I know that my true life purpose is to love myself and others, and to touch, move and inspire – to ignite the burning passion for life in people.

I am certain of my decision for it was approved by my trusted source. I can not go wrong. Life is all about choices and we are what we choose.

I made the choice – it's now or never. I refuse to die with my books inside of me. I will be able to make a true difference in the lives of others from my own uniqueness.

I'll leave you with these final thoughts: It is never too late to live your dreams no matter how bleak reaching them may appear, or how young or old you feel, or how far away the goal seems. You have to persevere, stay focused, and be purpose-driven.

I am truly happy for the life choices I have made. It was now or never and I can say, NOW is my time!

WILMA J. BROWN is on fire when it comes to training, speaking and touching the lives in her presence. As president and CEO of Wilma J. Brown & Associates, a personal and professional consulting and training organization, she is an enthusiastic go-getter with a passion for helping others. Visit www.WilmaJBrown.com to get your FREE report, *5 Tips to Success in Life*, and find out more about how she can ignite your passion for life with no alarm.

CHAPTER THIRTY

You Can Do Whatever You Want, Really!

MICHELLE COCHRAN, CC

~ Dedicated to the angel at the phone company ~

Every day I wake up, I thank God I did, and then I say out loud with a very big smile on my face, "I can do whatever I want," and I'll share with you why I feel this way.

I learned early in life that there are two definites and one possibility:

- Definite #1: God
- Definite #2: Your soul and its purpose
- The Possibility: Your life

I also learned that living deep inside of me was a knowing, a sense of inevitability that the drunken, abusive, neglectful circumstances I grew up in were not who I was. That there was something bigger than that – bigger than me – that I was here to do. That knowing and belief, and God, saved my life.

By age 16, I was homeless, tired, and depressed. I was driving in my beat-up, rusted-out Datsun, crying and screaming at God to either show me what to do or take my life, and I meant it. I had had enough.

Fortunately He didn't take me up on the latter, but He did show me what to do next.

I had a part-time job and a little money saved, so the next morning after my crying screaming meltdown, I found a local newspaper and started looking for a cheap place to rent. I found an ad for a studio apartment that was in the upper part of a house on the bad side of town. My first thought was, "No one is going to rent to a 16-year-old." But intuition said, "Call."

An elderly gentleman answered the phone and agreed to show me the apartment. You can imagine the look on his face when he saw how young I was, but he continued with the showing.

He was asking $200 dollars a month rent which I thought I could pay, so I asked him if I could please rent the apartment. He paused, and stared at me as if he was sizing me up in his mind. I said, "Sir, I know I'm young, but if you will just take a chance on me, I will pay my rent and I will take care of your apartment." He nodded and the place was mine.

After about a week, through working three jobs, I had saved enough money to get a phone. Frankly I was scared to death being in the apartment alone at night. So, I went to the neighbors to call the phone company to have one installed, but the lady from the phone company said, "I'm sorry I can't turn a phone on in your name as you have an outstanding balance of $500.00 on your account." I was taken aback, and asked, "How can that be? I have never had a phone before!" The words no sooner left my mouth when my heart sank. I knew that my mother had used my social security number to get a phone and had never paid the bill. I was so embarrassed. I said, "Ma'am, I am so sorry. I know what happened. My mother must have run this bill up in my name." With that, she put me on hold, and a moment later she came back on the line and said, "Honey, here is your new phone number. I've taken care of that for you."

I thanked her profusely, hung up, put my head down on that neighbor's kitchen table, and cried. To this day I cannot tell that story without crying. God was stepping in once again, showing me that when you have faith, let go and let God; He will always show up and meet your needs. This is the first step in true alignment, which allows you to function with certainty, not always fearless, but certain that there is no need to be afraid.

I believed in God, and in myself to be strong and keep moving forward, but my journey was filled with several more struggles and stories like that one. It seemed that even though I was blessed with the gift of keen awareness and the ability to see beyond my circumstances, I was left with this pesky little voice in my mind that loved to remind me that I was not worthy, not good enough. I self-sabotaged almost everything I tried to accomplish. I felt I wasn't worthy to know true wealth and success…but I didn't **believe** that, I only thought it. I often wondered how an opposite thought and belief could exist in the same body at the same time.

Then one day I read a book that explained the difference between ego and spirit and finally, click: total and complete alignment and freedom occurred within me. God, spirit, and mind – click, click, click. I got it. I finally had an explanation and language for all the negativity I was hearing in my mind, even though I knew that negativity was not who I was, or why I was here.

My whole life changed the moment I read A New Earth by Eckhart Tolle. I was able to distinguish between "mind trash" and my soul's purpose which made all the difference in my belief system.

For years I had a very successful travel and event-planning business that I loved, but after reading that book I discovered what profession had been calling to me for years, namely coaching. Helping other women silence their inner critic, own their power and worth, and show up boldly in an ever-changing and new world marketplace was my mission – to be the difference, to lead and assist them with the shift that is unfolding in our world. Today, I enjoy a thriving, successful business; healthy, incredible relationships; and new levels of wealth and freedom, all by choice and design. And so can you!

There is no difference between life and business; they are one and the same, part of the whole experience. Business is merely a tool and a vehicle for how you choose to express yourself and occur in the world. It allows you to expand in your purpose, gifts, and strengths, and to know success that is sustainable and defined by you**, your way**.

"I can do whatever I want" is my perfect reminder that God is running the show, and as long as I am in alignment with Him and use my business to be in service to humanity, in love and purpose, I can literally do and create whatever I want. Not to mention that that phrase is fun to say and evokes a sense of freedom and playfulness to BE out loud, and YOU can be and do whatever you want, too! Really!

Here are a few steps to help you on your path to align, expand, and succeed:

Align – To align is to have the ultimate "aha." It is when you are in a place of grounded peace and knowing that you are on purpose in God's service, and unattached to what happens or the outcome. It is allowing life to flow to and through you without judgment or fear. A simple willingness to say, "Yes," and step into what your intuition is telling you is right for YOU, no matter what the circumstances may look like. I ask you: Who rents an apartment to a 16-year-old? How often is a $500 phone bill randomly forgiven?

Expand – It's all about the energy! Have you ever walked into a room and there is someone who just seems to be the center of attention for some reason? They're no different than you, but there's just something about them – they're like a magnet. It's energy. When you can turn up the positive vibration in who you are being, it is like a magnet and, yes, it attracts your prospective clients! This is where YOUR personality is key, because you will always attract EXACTLY who you are meant to. YOUR personality is YOUR secret weapon – use it! Expand your energy in it! In my youth, I THOUGHT I had to constantly re-create myself to "fit" where I wanted to be accepted. Now I mold the universe to fit me through truth and authenticity. It's easier, refreshing, and much more productive.

Succeed – Know this: You ARE success, period. You're already there. Don't look for it, don't chase it, just decide you ARE success. If the negative mind trash shows up, just notice it and let it go.

The goals you set and meet along the journey of self-growth and expression, are often mistaken for success, but success is always who you are being, period. No more, no less – it's that simple. All that is left for you to do is to decide and define your "more." Decide what is the very next thing you want more of and then start today taking one action step towards it. Just know you cannot become successful, you can only BE success, AND you can do whatever you want. Really.

MICHELLE COCHRAN, CC, is a certified success and leadership coach, author, futurist, radio show host of Ladies Who Lead Radio on Blog Talk Radio, founder of The Lady Thought Leader Academy and More Life Events.com. Her greatest passion is to help others follow their joy, own their worth, and live their wealth, their way, through business. For a FREE subscription to her newsletter, *The Leader-zine,* visit www.LadyThoughtLeader.com.

CHAPTER THIRTY ONE

Climbing the Rock to Reach Your Entrepreneurial Dreams

LILI CRUCHELOW

I love a good challenge and this certainly fit the bill. Chimney Rock in the Wisconsin Dells area is on the highest bluff in lower Wisconsin, and I was going to climb it.

Challenging myself outside my comfort zone is something I have learned to be more open to doing. The feeling of accomplishing something new and reaching higher levels than I ever imagined is what inspires me.

I believe most people think that the status quo is acceptable and that living comfortably is a goal. I disagree. It takes more energy to hang on to these ideals than it takes to climb upward. We are capable of so much more than we realize and unless we take some chances and go for huge, inspiring goals, we will never know what we are capable of achieving.

In 2005, I was in turmoil over a decision I had to make. I could stay in a comfortable place working for a medical supply company where I earned $80,000 per year, or I could risk everything and start my own business.

I knew nothing about starting a business. I was trained as a nurse and had transitioned into medical sales, so at first I completely brushed the idea aside and did not give it a moment's consideration.

However, something inside of me started to burn: a desire to learn more about being an entrepreneur. I started to notice other entrepreneurs and found myself engaging them in conversation to learn more about starting a business. I began to think about the freedom and the challenge of building something by myself, for myself.

It was about six months from my first thought about starting a business until the moment the decision was made. My husband, Todd, and I were floating on the pool in our yard when he said, "Let's do it. We will always wonder 'what if' if we don't." From that moment we went into action. We mortgaged everything we owned, I quit my job, and our company, TLC Medical, was born. Our vision to do this was too strong to ignore and our passion too powerful to let die.

I've learned that the voices that try to keep you comfortable are built from your thoughts and life experiences. However, you can change your thoughts and you can change your experiences to build a vision of the life you want.

I believe everyone has a big inspiring dream or aspiration. It may be buried deep down inside them, but it is still there. It starts with belief. We are capable of doing everything that we "believe" we can.

Ten years ago I would have never been able to picture myself as an owner and operator of a multimillion dollar business or as an author, but now I couldn't imagine my life doing anything else.

I am building my business based on my vision which is a huge inspiring one. It keeps me excited and motivated to push forward even when I have no idea where forward is.

Looking up at Chimney Rock, I had that same sense of excitement. I could see the first few steps I would take, but from there the path was a mystery. The foot and hand holds were not visible and the peak looked like it was a mile away.

Harnessed in, with my friend holding onto the billet, I took the first few steps. Nerves kicked in big time. I was scared, but I knew I wanted to reach the top. I had to slowly start navigating my route. With each few steps, I would have to pause and look around to find the next spot that offered a solid hand or foot grip.

Every decision I made, every step I took, was all my own. I knew that no one was going to carry me to the peak of Chimney Rock. If I wanted to get there, I would have to do it on my own. Of course I had the support of my friends and family at the bottom cheering me on, but the climb was on me.

About two thirds of the way up the rock, I came to a point that appeared impassable. I had to maneuver myself to a point where I could maintain my position by holding on by just my fingertips and toes. I paused and looked up to the peak. I knew this was where I wanted to go, but I was stuck. I had to make a decision; I couldn't hold on for long as it was taking too much energy. It was either find a way up or give up and go back down. I was not about to give up. I knew that finding a foothold was possible and, with the knowledge of this fact, I knew I could find a way.

I held on to my position for a few minutes, moving a hand or a leg, testing the grips. There was nothing there. I found a big crack in the rock, but after several attempts I couldn't get a firm hold. The guide said we should use the crack by putting our arm all the way in it and bracing ourselves, using that leverage to push upward, but that seemed ridiculous and dangerous.

After standing there for a few minutes, I had to take a leap of faith and trust that this was the right decision. If I slipped with my arm stuffed into the crack, it would surely break my arm, but it was the move I had to make if I wanted to reach the top.

With full faith in my buddy Matt who was billeting me, I shoved my arm in the crevice, put a foot in a notch, and hoisted myself up into the base of the "v" of the crack. That was the move that assured my celebration at the top of Chimney Rock.

When I reached the summit I stood there for several minutes and reveled in the feeling of my accomplishment. I had taken on a task that looked to be impossible, and step by step I maneuvered and made choices that brought me to my goal.

I had believed I could get to the top. I didn't know how to do it, but I believed that I could. With that strong belief, a path appeared before me with each step I took.

Starting a business takes this same belief. It takes having an absolute conviction that you can reach your goal, no matter what. If you are hungry and inspired, if you take ownership of your results, and if you focus on what you want, nothing can stop you. Whatever may appear as an obstacle will easily be overcome as you approach and move through it.

I have built a very successful business that is growing and thriving, and the opportunities that are coming to me keep amazing me. I have taken on some hefty challenges and I have felt the rewards.

Having the willingness to reach for inspiring goals is the first step. I am also lucky enough to have a strong partner in my husband Todd, who lets me think of really crazy ideas and he supports each one of them. I believe this type of support is essential when building a business. Support can be found in your family and friends or in other recourses that you seek out. Continually talk to others in business and learn how they do things. Always be open to learning new ideas, and never get complacent. Constantly reach outside of your comfort zone.

Ask yourself these questions: What is it you really want? If there were no limitations and you could achieve your entrepreneurial dream, what would it be? Let yourself think of limitless possibilities. You do have an idea inside of you that just needs permission to be set free.

Let yourself think and dream about it. Start seeing yourself achieve that goal you desire. Feel the excitement, challenge, and freedom of controlling your own destiny. See the life that reaching this dream would provide for you. Just let it consume you so you really feel it. Once you truly let yourself believe in the possibility, the path will start to appear.

Success is inside of you. If you believe that you can climb the rock, the path upwards will start to appear with each step you take. You must believe, but you also must take action by taking the first step, no matter how small it is, and build from that.

It's those first steps that are the most important, because if you don't move outside of your comfort zone and take them, all you will have is an unfulfilled dream.

Open yourself up to big dreams and watch how the whole world changes!

LILI CRUCHELOW is the president and CEO of TLC Medical, a company she built from scratch to a multimillion dollar business in five years. She is author of *Climbing the Rock: An Entrepreneur's Guide to Reaching Your Dreams* and "Climbing the Rock" training programs designed to show aspiring entrepreneurs how to reach their dreams. Reach new heights in your entrepreneurial dream at www.ClimbingTheRockBook.com or visit www.LiliCruchelow.com.

CHAPTER THIRTY TWO

Banish Mind Chatter and Shift Into Balance Right Now!

KIT FUREY
JD, CHT, CEHP

Here I am. Surprised. Yet not surprised. When I heard, "You've achieved it. Now claim it," I knew my world at my very core had shifted. Permanently. "The mind once stretched never again returns..." I like knowing that. In my very bones I feel good... a sense of lightness, calm, clarity, balance. I've had an instant breakthrough.

Finally, I've let a massive backpack filled with limiting subconscious beliefs thud to the side of my path. Now as I move onward and upward, I can skip, dance, glide. Even leap. Or fly.

Looking back, I realize that changing the kind and quality of my inner questions moved me to this breakthrough. I'll help you do this, too! I'll guide you through an exercise to acquire a tool so you can experience a breakthrough – quiet your mind chatter, like "Am I enough?" "Am I worthy?" "Am I deserving?" "Am I okay?" Useless questions! Yes, you are enough, worthy, deserving. You are safe. End of discussion. Beware endless chatter – you're about to be silenced!

The gem awaiting you is among an array of tools I've acquired through dire necessity. At one period of my life I walked through a fire of overwhelming stress so consuming that I'd fall into bed at night exhausted, determined to gather enough energy during the dreamtime to miraculously rise like a phoenix come morning. You see, I was a single mother of three babes, one 18 months old and two three-year-olds, and going through a divorce, when I discovered my first-born struggles with special needs.

I shifted from full-time stay-at-home mom back to full-time work. I grieved for the daytime hours not spent with my children. I could share countless stories of bone-deep fear about not being a "good enough" mother; feelings of overwhelming stress, trying to balance livelihood and motherhood; gut-wrenching moments of despair when two, but not three of my children were invited to the same party. (When a precious child has been excluded, there's no good answer to the hurt and the question, "But not me?") And I had moments of near panic that work tasks would become a tsunami while I drove little ones to soccer practice or yet another therapy appointment.

Reflecting back, "overwhelming stress" doesn't even begin to describe how close to collapsing I felt most days. What did I want instead? Peace and a sense of equilibrium. Balance. I was determined to create that.

Clearly, a new set of inner tools was required. With them I knew I could whip myself into shape, keep the worlds of my little ones calmer, and maintain clarity, focus, and balance in my work. Each painful moment and all the tears and fears they spawned as I struggled were stepping stones for acquiring the tools to quell pain, fear, doubt, and grief... just for starters. Now I have the resources to quell all that – as a parent, in my business – in any area of my life.

I've been catapulted along a path to learn about the power of the other-than-conscious mind and how it limits **or** empowers us. I've been propelled to this moment, to share a tool with you, so you can start now to transform any mind chatter that haunts you or holds you hostage.

Would it be useful to stop asking yourself, "Am I good enough?" Or to stop being sideswiped by myriad thoughts that create fear, doubt, overwhelming stress, or other forms of "stuckness?"

There's a scientific basis for why the tool works to unravel subconscious beliefs and habits that create stuckness or other limitation. Without going into the science, I simply offer you a source-based powerful tool, if you feel called to experience it. Changing the quality of your inner dialogue can be simple and easy.

I offer this transformational tool because part of my purpose on this planet is to help make people's lives easier. I help people align their inner worlds of thoughts, beliefs, and emotions with how they choose to experience their outer worlds. People move from stuckness back into an easy, graceful flow of their essence.

Your chattering little ego mind probably has lots of questions about what this tool is, how it works, why it works, and will it work for you? I honor the fact that your ego mind has questions, and I gently set them aside in service of working directly with your higher consciousness, soul and source so you can accept your new "Align, Expand, Succeed" tool.

Let yourself know that your higher self will keep you safe, and that at your deepest and highest levels of self and soul, you already know everything you want to know. Your ego mind can just take a break for the next few minutes during this exercise as you allow your source to implement a great gift for you.

In the following exercise, your higher conscious, soul and source will be asking the right questions, rounding up your limiting beliefs, and gathering up resources from your future, ascending self. In short, they are doing everything and doing only what serves your divine ideal. I've offered a range of techniques for your higher consciousness and soul to use. I'm able to do this because your higher consciousness, soul and source are "outside of time." That's why this exercise is so safe and powerful.

I suggest you read the following exercise start to finish before you begin. This will go a long way toward putting your ego mind at ease. After you've read through the entire exercise, come back to the beginning of it, get a piece of paper and a pen, relax, and fully experience it as you follow the simple instructions.

To begin: Get comfortable and take a few deep breaths.

Ask yourself this question: "On a scale of 0-12, 12 being my divine ideal, 0 being the worst scenario I can imagine – far worse than I'll ever experience (be that pain, fear, doubt, feeling 'not good enough,' or some other experience of stuckness I want to shift) – when I think of my life as a whole, where am I now, 0-12?"

Just wait for the number you become aware of. You may see it, sense it, or just know it. Jot the number down now for future reference.

Now imagine a screen floating in front of you... a computer, TV, or movie screen, any kind of screen your heart desires. On that screen (even if you don't see or sense anything at all), the details of all the techniques I've asked be made available to your higher consciousness and soul; every shield against chaotic energy; every clearing process (especially those going after the limiting beliefs and patterns that create questions about being good enough, questions about whether you're worthy of life's great bounty and pleasures, whether you're deserving of all that you desire, whether you're safe and supported by "all that is"); every physical support process; every request for inspiration about your sacred path and purpose; all the details of everything I've focused on your behalf are being reflected to your higher consciousness and soul.

Anything I've requested that doesn't serve you has either been deleted or edited by your higher consciousness and soul.

Now ask the highest source of your being, by whatever word or name you use to refer to your source, if it is in divine alignment to implement everything on the screen for you.

When you sense that it is in divine alignment – and you will, because your source will only implement what serves you – just think or say "Yes!"

to accept everything on the screen. When you think or say "Yes!" then your source will implement everything with divine timing. (That could be the instant you say "Yes!" or some other time. Your source makes that judgment call.)

Take another deep breath and check back in by asking yourself, "On a scale of 0-12, where am I now?" And notice what's changed!

Now that you've looked at your screen and said "Yes!" your higher consciousness and soul can activate this tool any time you think or say, **"Align, Expand, Succeed!"** with the intent to clear your negative thoughts or feelings. You don't need to look at the screen again. **Simply think or say, "Align, Expand, Succeed!" with intent to shift your experience**. Then notice what's changed! You can use this tool whenever you want to shift your experience.

Godspeed and journey well.

Shifting from her formal training as a lawyer, *KIT FUREY* now helps people align their heads and hearts so they can reduce stress, serve more people and make inspired decisions in their personal and professional lives. She also teaches tools people can use to get themselves unstuck, fast and forever. Go to www.InstantBreakthroughSuccess.com and you'll get a FREE audio *Instant Breakthrough Session,* clear some very common limiting beliefs, and receive the Instant Breakthrough ezine.

CHAPTER THIRTY THREE

Surrendering to a
Conscious Way of Life

KATHLEEN GAGE

I grew up in a typical middle-class home: loving parents, the youngest of three girls, a solid religious foundation, never wanting for the necessities while enjoying a comfortable life. In spite of this, I made choices that placed me in turmoil, drifting from day to day with no clear purpose, having nowhere to call home, all the while mastering the art of being unemployable.

By my 25th year I hit the lowest point imaginable. Not sure how this happened, I was quick to blame everyone but myself for the lack to which I became accustomed. I was abusing various substances to ease the pain, yet the more I attempted to escape, the greater the pain got.

My daily mantra was, "God, not another day."

So, how did I go from this life of desperation to one in which I am blessed to do what I love, enjoying amazing abundance in all areas of my life, including clarity of mind and spirit?

I learned how to tap into an incredible source of energy that took me from a well-seasoned underachiever to an extremely high achiever.

This didn't happen overnight. Nor did it happen without a few bumps in the road; some minor, some major.

Having come from a place of complete lack, with ever-increasing success (or what I thought success should be) I experienced something I never imagined. I became fearful of losing everything only to return to a life of desperation.

The greater the fear, the harder I pushed for success. At one point that meant getting as many awards and recognitions possible. Yet nothing would fill the secret hole I felt in my gut.

I could never quite find the right combination that would bring me deep fulfillment. Sure, I was acquiring the outward indications of success such as money, community recognition, and the ability to buy a home and a nicer car, but inside there were unsettling feelings, mixed emotions and turmoil. I continually felt like I had something to prove to myself and to others – or so I thought. Part of the problem was basing my definition of success on what I thought it should be rather than what it really is (for me).

I have had shifts in my consciousness many times over the last three decades, but a big one came in my mid 40's, and another around the time I turned 50, and still another at 55.

Maybe it was that I had been immersing myself in various spiritual and religious teachings for so many years. Maybe it was maturity. Or maybe... just maybe... I had finally surrendered to what I am here to do: daily turn my life over to something greater than myself to be guided to my greater good, a good that allows me to live my life, both personally and professionally, in a very conscious manner.

After decades of searching, I now deeply understand we are all here for a reason. It's more than simply understanding, it's a knowing.

Our ego tries to convince us otherwise. Ego is what drives us to want more and more and more without recognizing we have it all right now.

So, what happened during those pivotal points? In a word, surrender. I had to admit things weren't working. I had to be willing to change. Surrendering and gaining clarity was not an overnight experience.

As I gained clarity, it became apparent that more change was in order.

It didn't have to be massive, it could be something as simple as taking a class at my local spiritual center. It could be changing my eating habits. It could be giving up an hour of television to pursue a passion or hobby. Each action would move me closer to my ideal of success, the definition of which had changed dramatically for me. It had become so simple that I released the need for any outward evidence.

Amazingly, the less I focused on the outward and concentrated on the inward – my heart, my soul, my spirit, and my teachings – the outward began to take care of itself. I was surrounded by abundance on numerous levels. And life became very simple. Not always easy, but very simple.

Regardless of what we believe, there are times our beliefs are put to the test. Just when we think we have it all figured out we likely have more to learn.

About ten years ago, I suspended operations in my business to run a career development company in Salt Lake City. I was one of the primary decision makers in the company, had the corner office, a wonderful staff, a great income, stock options, and a handsome bonus structure.

I had arrived. Or so I thought. The first year was fantastic. My team and I were accomplishing some amazing feats. Revenues went up by nearly 80%, client satisfaction went from mediocre to fantastic, the company name was being talked about in lots of circles, and the future looked bright. That is until I discovered the owner was using very unscrupulous practices to secure investment dollars for another company that was very closely connected to the one I was running.

When I confronted the owner about what he was doing, his response was, "Kathleen, you need to grow up and realize this is how business is run."

This was during the time many large corporations were going through major collapse. It was incredible to realize I was smack in the middle of a similar situation only on a smaller scale.

The owner indicated that if I just kept things to myself I could continue to get the paycheck, keep the office, enjoy the perks, and bask in the prestige. I was appalled and frightened. Here I thought I had arrived. I had what I thought success was, and yet it was all a scam. I felt like a total fraud. How could I have been so blind?

I was confronted with my truth. Stay with the company and live a lie, deceiving countless people, or leave and go completely into the unknown with no guarantee of what came next.

I left, and although things were tough for a period of time, it was the most honorable thing I could have done. The most difficult part of the situation was the anger and old thinking that came up.

Yet the difference between my life during those decades and my life after I left the security of that job was like night and day. I now had tools such as prayer, meditation, and a connection to my source that had been nonexistent in my twenties. All I needed to do was be willing to use them.

It didn't take much for me to become very willing to implement what I had learned, which was that when I am able to surrender to what life has in store, there are many surprises awaiting.

I also learned that it is during times of great uncertainty that we are gifted with opportunities to discover more about who we are than we ever dreamed possible.

Everyone goes through periods when we are literally stopped in our tracks. Times when we are confronted with who we claim to be. Times when we either honor our truth or stuff it, only to become a bit more unconscious with each passing day.

The choice to leave the company set in motion a series of events that have landed me where I am today. Getting through the uncertainty deepened my faith, trust, and inner knowing that everything always works out when I allow it to. It also allowed me to travel a path to where I now have an extremely successful career doing what I love with people I enjoy working with. It allowed me to shift priorities to know that I don't have to chase success. I simply have to allow it.

According to the Law of Attraction, we invite everything, absolutely everything, into our experiences. This is often misunderstood to mean that we manifest specific details of negative experiences.

For example, I had been training for a marathon shortly after my 55th birthday when I broke my ankle. This accident set in motion a series of events that allowed me to respond to my circumstances differently than I might have otherwise, and I am forever grateful for the deeper experience this brought me – one that I had never dreamed possible.

Based on the Law of Attraction, did I ask for the broken ankle, or did the broken ankle give me the deeper experience I sought? I daresay the latter.

When I broke my ankle, some were quick to say, "You failed. You didn't complete your goal. You're not going to participate in the marathon."

Not so. My goal has merely been redefined so that I may know more fully **what I am being called to be**. Notice I did not say called to do. Sometimes we are not meant to "do" anything more than stop, reflect, and take the next indicated step. Then we can more consciously and joyfully do what we are called to do, personally and professionally.

Through it all, the greatest lesson has been that of surrender. For it is in the surrender we are more fully able to live a conscious way of life that we can be proud of.

KATHLEEN GAGE, of The Street Smarts Marketing, is an internet marketing advisor who works with spiritually aware entrepreneurs who are ready to turn their information into moneymaking products and services. Kathleen is best known for her expertise with teleseminars, online book launches, information product development and continuity programs. She is committed to helping others discover how their life's work and spiritual path go hand in hand. Visit www.KathleenGage.com and www.DailyAwareness.com to learn more.

CHAPTER THIRTY FOUR

Is This Heartburn or the Calling of My Soul?

LYNNE KLIPPEL

Back in 2006, my life was a mess. I'd opened a business in 2002 and was losing money almost as fast as I made it. I loved my work coaching others, but had trouble marketing my work, charging appropriate fees, and attracting a steady stream of clients. While clients raved about my work as a coach, as a business owner I felt inept.

I held on to my day job and prayed every night that my business would grow so I'd be able to fulfill my dream of working from home. My bedroom sitting area was full of visualization boards. I had sticky notes with affirmations posted all over my house and my car, and I'd read so many business and spiritual books that my head swam.

After attending numerous seminars and coaching programs, and devouring home study courses, I was stumped. Why was I failing at my passion? What did other people know that I couldn't figure out? Should I give up on this silly dream and refocus my goals on climbing the corporate ladder?

Things on the home front weren't too good either. My husband had been out of work since 2001, first from a layoff and then from a serious illness. The doctors advised that he not return to the workforce. He was will-ing to be a "house husband," but that left the burden of being the primary breadwinner for our family of five on my shoulders. Our marriage was already shaky from five years of financial troubles, stress, and worry. My family and friends thought I was unrealistic about my business goals and should be thankful for my secure corporate job and great health insurance.

A woman I knew kept inviting me to a free call on Tuesday nights with a spiritual teacher who talked about prayer and meditation. I said no for about a year. I already had a church home, was active in my faith, and had read countless books on spirituality. Besides, my vision boards, affirmations, and prayers had not worked, so I figured nothing else would help me either.

Finally, one Tuesday in February of 2006, I gave in and attended the call. I was depressed and thought that at least listening in on this free phone call might lift my spirits for an hour or so.

A very strange thing happened. All during the call, my heart felt hot. I didn't think I was having a heart attack, but wondered what was going on. I loved the meditation exercise and felt the teacher was speaking directly to me during the entire call. It seemed like she knew me and how hard I'd been struggling in all the aspects of my life.

At the end of the call, an invitation was made to attend a ten-day spiritual retreat in Mexico that summer with this teacher at a place near Guadalajara. The topic would be stress reduction and how to live a happy and successful life. My heart started to jump in my chest and I broke out in goose bumps. Even though it made no sense at all, I knew that I was supposed to attend that retreat.

This was crazy. I was already in debt, working a full time job, had three kids and a sick husband at home, and was trying to build a business. How in the world would I find the time and money to travel to a foreign country with a group of people I did not know? Would there be strange chanting or sitting in a lotus position for hours on end? I was a Midwestern farm girl from a conservative background with a degree from a Bible college. Was I getting sucked into a cult?

All through the next day, my heart felt strangely warm and expansive. I had millions of questions going around in my mind, but my heart felt sure that I was to go on this trip. I told my husband we needed to find a bunch of money because I just had to go on this spiritual adventure. To his great credit, he just said that if it was important to me, I should go.

A few months later I set off for central Mexico, scared to death and deeply excited at the same time. For the next ten days I'd be retreating with a group of women I'd never laid eyes on at a vegetarian resort miles from the nearest airport. I was not sure what I was more scared of: eating only vegetables for ten days, being far away from home in a place where I did not speak the language, or spending ten days without any phone or internet connection. This was one of the biggest risks I'd ever taken.

The first night there was chanting! I got the giggles.

The entire week was filled with strange and wonderful adventures. There were workshops filled with laughter and learning, soaks in pools of warm mineral spring water, hikes, sparkling conversations, and a trip to meet a local shaman who did a ceremony for us in his healing cave. I ate sliced cactus in my scrambled eggs each morning and liked it. I even had my body covered in volcanic mud in a healing treatment. I giggled through that too.

By the end of the retreat, I felt reborn. I had new friends who seemed like sisters, a new sense of direction for my life and my business, and a deeper connection with my faith and spiritual core.

Since then my life and my business have improved so much that at times I have to pinch myself. The stressed, worried, and depressed woman I was back in 2006 has disappeared, replaced by a woman who is happy, peaceful most of the time, and successful.

My life was transformed because the trip to Mexico taught me some very valuable lessons. First, I learned how to manage stress effectively by using simple tools like daily meditation, deep breathing, journaling, and getting more rest.

I also learned how important it is for me to do new things and get out of my comfort zone. Life can get stale and lose its zest when the focus is always on work and responsibilities, and when there is a lack of adventure in our daily living.

Attending a spiritual retreat, away from computers, phones, and modern life, has become my yearly gift to myself. Each time that I take a week to renew my spirit, rest, connect with others, and learn more about how to live a happy, peaceful life, my business grows and my life improves. A retreat provides time of quiet contemplation and refreshment that is essential for my well-being.

The most important thing I learned on my adventure in Mexico is that when my heart is burning, it's the voice of my soul, nudging me to follow my intuition, take a risk, trust, and expand my vision of what's possible.

So, what about you?

How long has it been since you really listened to the voice of your soul?

You may not be able to fly off to Mexico for a ten-day retreat. However, you can try these simple techniques at home to begin expanding your connection with your spirit:

1. Give yourself a mini-retreat day. Pick a place in your home town or the surrounding area and spend a day on your own. You may want to go on a hike, visit a museum or botanical garden, sit by a river, or go to a cathedral. Include a picnic or a great lunch in a place you've never been before. To make this day meaningful, don't use your cell phone, spend at least part of the day outdoors, and take only your journal or sketch book. Focus on doing things you've never done before, enjoying peace and quiet, and savoring a day of relaxation. Try to do this at least quarterly. Whenever you feel totally overwhelmed, retreat, even for a few hours.

2. Slip times of meditation into every day. Find a few minutes several times each day when you can breathe deeply, clear your mind, and slow down. Learn to listen to your intuition by stopping your busy mind and turning inward. Find a way to incorporate times of meditation and prayer into each day and notice that you become more centered, less reactive, and able to think more clearly.

3. Be open to the idea that sometimes your heart knows better than your head. Practice following the urging of your intuition. Pay attention to the results. Soon you will find that your life and your business are improving every day.

As you find new ways to become more peaceful, you will see your life and your business expand. Miracles will start to occur. New opportunities and connections will arrive at just the right time.

You will giggle, not from embarrassment, but from joy. And you just might learn to like cactus with your scrambled eggs!

LYNNE KLIPPEL, bestselling author and publisher, has coached aspiring authors from six of the seven continents to write books and use them to build their business. As a lifelong bookworm, she is thrilled to spend her days reading manuscripts, publishing books, coaching, teaching, and hosting her radio show, BookBitesTalkradio.com. If you have a book inside you, let Lynne help you by downloading her FREE information kit at www.FreeBookResources.com.

CHAPTER THIRTY FIVE

Be True to You...
No Matter What

CHRISTINE KLOSER

It was mid-2009 when I woke up from a dream. In the dream, I appeared to be at the height of my career. I was a successful author, coach and publisher, a well-known expert in my field, making great money, and having a positive impact on thousands of entrepreneurs around the world. I worked hard to do everything everyone suggested in my business. I attended all the right workshops, learned all the new strategies, and implemented them one by one in my business. I was well-respected and had a fantastic network of friends, colleagues and partners. People knew my name.

Sounds like a great dream, doesn't it? Perhaps it's a dream that you aspire to achieve in your journey of conscious entrepreneurship.

There was only one problem... what appeared to be a dream felt like a nightmare inside. Yes, I was really living everything stated in my dream above. On the outside it all looked "perfect." But inside of me, things didn't feel the same.

You may be asking how that could be so? After all, I am a pioneer in the field of conscious entrepreneurship. In fact, many people credit me with the popularity of this term itself. But how could I be living that externally fantastic, conscious, aligned life and also be feeling constantly stressed, overwhelmed, frustrated, and under so much self-inflicted pressure?

It's easy to see how in hindsight. I was only 90% conscious in my business. It was the 10% of unconsciousness that caused the inner turmoil.

For years, I forged forward at 90%. Hey, let's face it, 90% isn't all that bad. Many people out there get through life on a lot less than that, so I must be doing okay if I'm 90% conscious. I'm way ahead of the game! Or so I thought.

The truth is 90% consciousness and 10% unconsciousness is a major growth opportunity waiting to happen. It's impossible to walk the path of a conscious entrepreneur 90% of the time and not have it come back to bite you in the bottom.

I got bitten big time, and I'm sharing it with you so you can learn from my mistakes and not make them yourself. The biggest mistake I made in my journey was paying more attention to what other people said I should do than what I felt inside. For example, everyone in my world at the time was offering super high-end VIP coaching programs. Someone suggested I do the same thing.

I allowed the unconscious 10% of me to decide that, sure, I "should" do that too. After all, everybody else is and why not me? So I didn't listen to the whisper in the background of my mind saying, "Something about this isn't right." I was 90% on board with it and 10% feeling an inkling that this wasn't the most aligned direction for me.

Well, I ignored the 10% that felt something wasn't right and offered a high-end VIP coaching program. It launched with success as my first new client signed up in a matter of days.

Anyway, without sharing all the details, I'll tell you that this program, once it was up and running, presented the most challenging time I've ever faced in my business or my life. Through this experience, any issues I'd ignored on an emotional, spiritual, and financial level were brought to the surface for purification and healing.

I began to ask myself questions at a deeper level, allowed myself to look past what I'd always seen as true about myself, and questioned if it was really true... or not. I allowed myself to look beneath it all, to look behind the external success, and look deep into my heart.

What I discovered to be the truth was that I was being called – called to "uplevel" and realign at a depth I never had before. I was being called by the universe to walk this path of 100% consciousness so I could help others do the same. I was (and still am) called to get messy, to uproot decades-old patterns that no longer served me, to stretch way out of my comfort zone, to feel the shakiness of the ground beneath me, to trust like I never have before, to be more authentic, to release my old self-identity and surrender to a higher spiritual calling.

But in this process of being called, I continue to face the unconscious 10%. I recommit everyday to having an intimate understanding of the false beliefs that have run me... so I can release them and not repeat old patterns. And beyond that, to help and serve others through my experience.

So, to help you right now, I want to share some of the false beliefs I let run the unconscious 10%. I share these with you with the prayer that if you recognize any of these voices in yourself you will do the work and get the guidance and help you need to heal and transform them.

The voices I let run the unconscious 10% of my decisions sounded something like this: "I'm not enough. I have to prove myself. I don't deserve to be truly successful. People will only value me if I make money. Nobody cares who I AM, they only care about what I DO. I have to be perfect. I should do what works for everyone else. I'll never get it right. I have to work hard. I don't have enough time, etc."

I need to breathe for a moment as I write this. And, I'd encourage you to breathe deeply right now, too. It's not pleasant to admit to myself (and to you) that some of these voices run the unconscious 10% of me.

Yet I hear the much louder voice right now telling me that being open, vulnerable, truthful and honest about my own journey as a sometimes "unconscious conscious entrepreneur" will serve many people – people who are having this conversation with themselves silently, while trying to hold up an image to the outside world that doesn't match what's happening inside. It's exhausting and scary to be in that place, which is why I'm sharing my experience so you can be free of it.

The benefits of being willing to look deeper, to see where you've been unconscious and allow those things to come to light, is worth every ounce of energy it takes to face them and admit how they've impacted you… and those around you.

This is a time of great global awakening – a time when we are shifting from a paradigm of greed, competition, and scarcity, to one of generosity, cooperation, and abundance. So, as a conscious entrepreneur yourself, the only way to truly make YOUR contribution to this great shift is to make this shift within yourself. It's time for YOU to do the internal work to free yourself from the pains of this old paradigm, and to step 100% into the paradigm within yourself that you want to see in the world.

It all comes down to truth: learning to be truthful with yourself, learning to share your truth with others, and learning to walk in truth 100% of the time. This is what makes the difference in the journey of the "unconscious conscious entrepreneur" and that of the "fully-conscious conscious entrepreneur."

I invite you now to say YES to being fully conscious, and to remember this commitment to yourself when seeing the truth about a part of yourself that is painful. Just the truth that you are a person who is reading these words right now is a confirmation that YOU were meant to hear this message and to live by it as you join in the great GLOBAL realignment. This is who you are; this is the power you have; this is who the world needs you to be.

CHRISTINE KLOSER is a spiritual guide for conscious entrepreneurs. At her "Freedom Retreats" she helps entrepreneurs transform from "doing" to "being" in their business, (and their life). Through her publishing company, she leverages the experience of writing, publishing, and marketing a book to help entrepreneurs access their truth and share it with the world in an impactful way. Join Christine for FREE group coaching to awaken to your truth at www.MyWakeUpWednesday.com.

CHAPTER THIRTY SIX

Darkness to Light, Failure to Success, Bottom to Top: One Woman's Path From the Depths to Alignment, Expansion and Success

CAROL LIEGE

FROM DARKNESS TO LIGHT

Washington, D.C., September 9, 1985 – My story opens on a dreary day in a Marriott hotel, alone, sitting with my head between my knees, praying for guidance about what choice to make: leave my alcoholic husband and pull my life together, or go to a rehab center. I knew my drinking was out of control.

"If you'll help me help my children, God," I begged, "I'll do what I can to help other women overcome this same terrible situation we're in."

The phone rang. A friend from Texas I hadn't seen in many years drawled, "Caaarol? This may sound crazy, but ah think ah had a vision. At least, ah saw a picture of you sitting in a dark room with your head between your knees, and heard a voice tell me to call you. Ah got your number from yer husband. Are you alright?"

Then she said the voice ("Ah promise I don't usually talk like this, Caaaarol") told her to give me a message: "Open the door. The light is in the hall."

"What kind of message is that?" I asked impatiently. "How does that help me know what to do?"

Later that day I made my decision, opened the door, and eureka! Of course, there was light in the hall. "So what?" I wondered. Was it a sign? What did it mean?

FROM TOP TO BOTTOM TO TOP

I had been married nearly twenty years. I had sunk from being a valedictorian, class president, top graduate student, psychiatric social worker, youngest supervisor, statewide mental health program planner, high-level government professional, and senior national public affairs consultant to becoming a chain-smoking, nasty, sloppy drunk on the verge of getting fired.

My husband, once a prominent medical researcher, had lost prominent university and government jobs because of his drug use and drinking, and was working as a counterman in a pizza parlor. We were paying the bills only because we'd made good investments in the days when we were sober and sane. We had hit the bottom, and my husband wasn't open to change. He wasn't even open to admitting we both drank too much.

He drank and did drugs even before we were married. I didn't. It took several years for me to fully engage in his world, and then only because my conservative Midwestern values said I was supposed to put my family first and always support my husband, who claimed I was "boring" because I didn't join in his "recreations."

By now (1985), I was definitely worse off than he was. While I was still managing to hold on to a pretty prominent job (barely), I was actually more addicted, more dysfunctional, more disgusting, and far more desperate than he.

I believed (probably incorrectly) I could change if I just got away from him, but decided the safer course was to go to inpatient chemical dependency treatment at Hazelden, where first lady Betty Ford had gone. Hazelden is in Minnesota, in my family's hometown, and a place where there are public awards and rallies to celebrate people who have overcome chemical dependency and addiction.

My first night at Hazelden, a speaker shared her earlier experience as a patient there. "I wasn't sure I belonged here," she said. "Then the first night there was a kind of miracle. I looked out over the lake, and above it I saw a door with light shining out from behind. I opened the door, and in the light there I saw my alcoholism. I knew then I was in the right place."

That affirmation, along with the spiritual development steps I learned there, started me on a purposeful journey to align my life with the promise I had made to a higher power, a voice, the universe, God as I understood God – an understanding which has changed during the subsequent years of my journey but remained steadfast. My Purpose, with a capital P, became to find out how to help myself and my children build successful, fulfilling lives, and then to inspire and enable other women to do it. I thought of my life as a research project; I suppose all lives really are.

FAST-FORWARD TWENTY-FIVE YEARS

It's now twenty-five years later, and it's been quite a journey. I now drink bubbly water. I did divorce my husband, then helped him get addiction treatment, and he's been a successful university professor and administrator for many years. I got my daughters treatment when they needed it, and today they're both successful adults with lovely homes, wonderful children, and good careers, although they still have their own challenges stemming from their difficult childhoods.

During these last twenty-five years, I've started several businesses, some successful, some not so much. I've done research, planning, consulting, coaching, coalition building, developed new organizations and associations for others, invested in real estate, invested in the stock market, rehabbed foreclosures, marketed other people's products, done internet marketing, sold crafts and even taught sewing. Today, I feel I'm at the top of my game.

For most of these years, my family's recovery and success – its journey from the bottom to the top – has remained my highest priority. Not just for me or them, but for you – and for God. My life continues to be a research project, experimenting with what works and what doesn't, which self-help books and programs make sense and which don't, what treatment programs are appropriate for different kinds of addictions and abuses that affect families and children, and other practical matters that would be useful for other women to know if they find themselves dealing with situations like ours.

FAILURE TO SUCCESS

I moved to California in 1998 and was amazed to hear women business owners there discussing their spiritual lives and asking whether they were "on purpose" at professional networking meetings. Back in Boston and Washington, where I'd spent all my working years up until then, they would have given me a little white coat for Christmas if I'd discussed things like that!

That same year I attended the First International Conference on Spirituality and Business in New York, and started networking with people who were promoting "conscious business" nationally. Suddenly the private, personal practice I'd started back in 1985 ("We strive to maintain conscious contact with God, praying only for knowledge of His will for us and the power to carry it out.") expanded into my business world and found support there, as well as providing me with opportunities to help and mentor others.

While in California, I helped form several women's business groups affiliated with national organizations, including a Professional Women's Roundtable, affiliated with the National Association of Female Executives;

the Women's Leadership Forum, affiliated with The International Alliance; and the California chapter of the U.S. Women's Chamber of Commerce. These groups were filled with women building conscious businesses and overcoming problems. It was a glorious environment for my personal and business growth and expansion. Later, I moved into private real estate and securities investing.

I recently took off a year to spend in the town where my children live, helping them with their lives and children. That was my intention, at least.

I did help a great deal in a day-to-day sense, doing things like babysitting, housesitting, chauffeuring, paying for things, but hindsight is 20/20 and only time will tell if I did more good or harm. I did my best. I surfaced old issues hoping to resolve them, tried to change patterns my children learned in that dysfunctional home, confronted their own drinking, and suggested "healthy family" self-help books. Mostly they got mad at me for this and told me to "Live and let live," but things look to me like they're moving in a better direction now. Five or ten years from now will be a better time to judge. So I agree: it's time to let go and let God.

That year over, my intuition said it was time to think about what I could do to help other women living with tough problems. When I then received an invitation to participate in preparing this book, I took it as an affirmation – a sign the time had come to keep my 1985 promise:

"If you'll help me help my children, God, I'll do what I can to help other women overcome this same terrible situation we're in."

My talent has always been finding and analyzing information, synthesizing it, summarizing it, and communicating it in understandable and common sense ways that can lead to effective action. That's what I excelled at as a state planner, public affairs consultant, coalition builder, conscious businesswoman, business leader, and even as an investor. I believe that's what a lot of women in troublesome situations really need: good information and recommendations from the best resources, analyzed and summarized in ways that are easy to understand and suggest doable actions to take, and someone to cut through all the crap and tell them what they can do – what they need to do – in simple terms anyone can understand.

So, I started a new business project, still nameless as this goes to press, which will provide you, the conscious woman, with the best resources, information, education, support and suggestions we can find to help you deal with whatever troublesome situations you, your family, your friends, or employees may face today or tomorrow. I have bright, enthusiastic young women interviewing world experts and researching our initial priorities right now. Please feel free to contact us and let us know what YOU think our priorities should be!

If you're one of the women still in the dark today, I hope we'll soon be able to open a new door for you, and show you some light in the hallway beyond.

CAROL LIEGE has been a psychiatric social worker, national public affairs consultant, business owner, real estate investor, writer, and infopreneur. She is now launching a new conscious business project to empower and equip women with the best resources and advice available for overcoming the toughest problems in their lives, families, and businesses. Go to www.CarolLiege.com to weigh in on the problems you'd like to see covered, and receive their first report FREE when it becomes available.

CHAPTER THIRTY SEVEN

This is the Perfect Time to Be An Entrepreneur!

LAUREN MCMULLEN

Did you know we are living in the perfect time to become an entrepreneur? Here is a short history lesson to explain why:

There has been a global shift in how people communicate with each other and it has changed the way they think as well. This may actually be the biggest change in how we humans communicate with each other since the invention of the printing press!

I know those are big words, but think about it. Before the printing press, books were incredibly expensive and the common people could not afford them, so most never learned how to read. The aristocracy and the church controlled the masses. People had absolutely no power nor any idea what the laws were.

When Gutenberg invented the printing press in 1440, it led to the first mass production of books in history, and slowly they became more common. First the Bible was printed, then text books, and finally literature books. This invention was actually the catalyst for the change experienced from the Middle Ages to the Renaissance period.

The global shift that is going on right now started about six or seven years ago with the emergence of the social networks. As their popularity spread slowly across the internet, web 2.0 (which just means content that is interactive on the World Wide Web) became the norm. People shifted their perspective as well. The change began with the younger generation, of course, but now there are no boundaries of age, sex, or economic condition. Almost everyone who is online has accessed these social media sites at some time or another.

The social networks were built on the philosophy of creating connections and starting conversations between users. Those conversations lead to people developing relationships and building their own online community. Community has always been a basic human need, but it has been neglected over the last 20 years or so because most people are just too busy with their own family and work to build outside relationships. Social networks have now spread around the globe and they are used by people of all nationalities and demographics!

But enough history. Let's go back to my first question: "Why this is the perfect time to become an entrepreneur?"

Along with socializing, the social networks have become the natural place for business people to network. Savvy marketers have figured out that they can use the social networks to market their products and services, so long as they take the time to develop a relationship with the people in their target market first.

This kind of marketing has been around since the beginning of time. It is called "word of mouth marketing," and studies show that word of mouth marketing is 3 to 4 times more likely to be successful than traditional forms of marketing.

Traditional marketing relies on things like overinflated promises, hype, and imagined scarcity, and it is interruption-based. Word of mouth marketing is relationship and permission based, so it is a perfect fit for the social networks.

Because of the incredible reach of the internet, simple word of mouth marketing becomes word of mouth marketing on steroids!

Even big businesses have jumped on the social media marketing bandwagon. Many of them are using it to successfully generate sales, as long as they are careful to play by the rules. Social media has also changed people's expectations. Consumers now expect to engage with the brands who want their business. It's not unusual to have an actual conversation with the CEO of Zappos on Twitter today!

Please don't give up on me. I am getting to the entrepreneur part, I promise. I just needed to set the stage first.

I am sure we can agree there has been a lot of financial upheaval in recent years. The failing banks and the mortgage crisis have caused many people to lose their jobs, their retirement savings, and even their health care. This could be a bleak picture, but in many cases a different one has emerged. It turns out that many of those displaced workers had a dream to be an entrepreneur, but were always a little afraid to take that first step.

Out of desperation, many of them had to look for another way to support themselves and their families and they noticed the power of the internet! They began to look at where their passion lay, and then wondered if they could make their passion profitable. Some figured out how they could position that passion into an online business. Social media marketing then became the obvious vehicle for spreading the word about their business around the world!

I know you have heard that necessity is the mother of invention, but I like to say adversity is often the mother of invention. That has certainly been the case in my situation. I was one of those people whose life was thrown into upheaval by circumstances beyond my control.

My calm, carefree life was turned upside down about five years ago when my husband of over 30 years was diagnosed with an unusual autoimmune kidney disease. The doctors said there was no cure, no proven treatment, and they predicted his kidneys would fail within five years. (So far he has managed to beat those odds!) Almost overnight he became disabled. It did not take long for medical bills to exhaust all of our retirement savings, and it became obvious that I needed to get a job or we would need to downsize drastically and move away from our family home in the country.

When this happened, I had not worked outside the home for over fifteen years. I had been blessed with the luxury of staying on our little farm in middle Tennessee where I played at raising horses, volunteered at a handicapped riding program, and managed the Helping Hands Ministry at my church. We lived over 75 miles from any city large enough to provide good income opportunities, plus I really had no recent employment history that would make me hirable anyway.

After lots of prayer and much soul searching, I turned to something I have always loved, which was the internet, and I found my passion! I had a marketing background, so my passion turned out to lie in social media marketing. I invested in the necessary training online and I have been able to create a profitable business in about three years' time.

Now I get to help other entrepreneurs learn how they too, can leverage social media to market themselves and their businesses online. Plus the added bonus is I am having a blast!

My advice to you is this: If you have been impacted by the recent financial meltdown, then it is the perfect time for you to become an entrepreneur as well. What are you waiting for? Find your passion, create your product or service, and then position yourself as an expert on the internet so you, too, can become a profitable entrepreneur just like me.

LAUREN MCMULLEN, social marketing specialist, is the owner of the virtual assistant practice Time Finder 4 You. She is passionate about social media and how it has revolutionized the way business owners can communicate with their prospects, clients and customers. Visit www.TimeFinder4You.com to sign up for her "Social Media Video Tips" series and find out more about how she can help you learn to leverage social media marketing for more sales of your products and services online.

CHAPTER THIRTY EIGHT

Generosity is a Business Strategy

CHRISTIAN MICKELSEN

Every conscious business owner relies on doing well in sales and marketing in order to succeed. The marketing brings in the leads and sales bring in the income. But many entrepreneurs don't excel in sales and marketing because they think it's pushy, or it feels weird to try to get someone to buy something.

What would you say if I told you there's a little-known business strategy that's really fun, feels great, and can help you skyrocket your sales and your income? You'd want to know what it is, right? So here it is: Give away so much that it scares you! Yes, GIVE away so much that it scares you. Here's what I mean by that.

Unfortunately, a lot of people are afraid to give too much because they don't want to "give away the store." The strategy here isn't necessarily about how much you give, (although you can certainly give a lot more than most entrepreneurs realize), but it is about giving away your best stuff. Stay with me here. A lot of times people don't want to give away what they think is their super, super secret best stuff because they're afraid that people won't want to buy whatever it is they are selling. The thinking is that if they receive the good stuff free then they won't have a need to buy from you.

But in this day and age there is so much value you can create, that there are always opportunities to create more value and serve in a new way, so you'll never run out of offerings for your prospects and clients. Ask yourself this question now: "How can I add more value?"

If you believe in an abundant, infinite universe (which I bet you do if you're reading this book), it would serve you to come from a place of having infinite value, infinite resources, and infinite products and services that you can offer to your clients and customers. If this is true, then you won't ever run out of things to offer or sell through your business. If you do give away "your best stuff," or at least the stuff that would make the best impact on people in the shortest amount of time, it really sets you up to succeed. People will say, "Oh wow! If that's the free stuff then the paid stuff must be even better!" and they will be more likely to invest in your products and programs.

However, it can be a little scary to give away something so valuable. On a personal note, during one of my recent launches, I gave away something that initially I was scared to consider. Let me explain so you have an example of how this strategy of generosity really works so you can model it in your own business.

I was doing a launch for my program called "Free Sessions That Sell." In the program I teach people how to sign up clients from a free coaching session: you give away the free session and then through the process of coaching them you get clients to sign up at the end of the call.

I teach the step-by-step system in a program that sells for $2,000. The give-away for this launch was the entire step-by-step script for how to do the free session. I call it the "Free Sessions That Sell Roadmap."

After seriously doubting I could get through the fear of giving away the script, I decided to heed my own words and be generous! Well, people loved it. I got more comments on my blog for this freebie than anything we have ever done before. Our sales were really good, too, generating multiple six figures in one week. Generosity really works as a practical and profitable business strategy!

So, for anyone asking themselves the question, "If I give the good stuff away how will I still make money?" you'll see by my personal example that you really will.

Another benefit of being really generous and giving away your best stuff is that it helps you build a tribe of people that are a good fit for what it is that you offer. Being generous and building a tribe puts you in a position of taking on a stewardship over that group of people.

One of the ways to check in with yourself to see if you are taking on stewardship is to be honest and find out if you've been asking the question, "How can I market to them?" or "How can I serve them?" For me, personally, I have taken on stewardship of a group of coaches and consultants who are working to grow their business and help more people. Once I identified this group, I decided not only to create things to sell to them, but I was committed to creating products and services that were going to be of service to them. I even designed my marketing materials so they would be helpful to coaches. Basically, everything I do is in keeping with providing greater service to the personal and professional coaching industry. Even my sales letters have techniques and tips in them. A lot of times entrepreneurs who market online just have a sales letter that sells stuff, but mine are designed so that they teach, too!

So, how about you? Can you be more generous with the group of people you want to serve? If so, in what ways can you provide more value to help them?

To help you understand this philosophy more deeply, I want to share with you my personal experience when I was starting out in business. You'll see what a difference being generous can make.

During my first few years as a coach, I struggled and fell behind on my mortgage over and over again. I would get some clients, lose some clients, get some clients, lose some clients, and it was really a tough time. (Thank goodness I was at least doing something I was really passionate about and something that I really loved.)

I was trying to learn everything I could to get clients, and a lot of it just felt really uncomfortable – very unnatural, even slimy. It didn't feel like anything I would like to do and it certainly wasn't the way I would want to be marketed and sold to.

Thankfully, one of my role models early on was Thomas Leonard, who unfortunately passed away seven years ago. He generated so many ideas and would create little things to give away to those on his list all the time.

That was my first taste of seeing generosity in action... and that it could actually work! So, I modeled it a little bit in the early days and quickly realized how good I felt using this model. I just couldn't do it any other way and still feel good about it. Over the years, I've continued to notice great results.

Now keep in mind that you do have to find a balance between being generous and smart marketing that ensures people see the value in what you are offering. It wouldn't serve anyone, least of all you, if you under-valued what it is you do offer. The good common sense marketing strategy of making it easy for others to see the benefits and value of what you're offering is still very important. You always want to lead with your product or service benefits, even when you're giving something away. Making the value crystal clear and being generous with what you give away is a tried and true recipe for success.

But beyond any business-related result you'll experience through generosity is the impact your generosity can have on the world. Imagine your seed of generosity growing and expanding in a way that has a ripple effect on others. I know a lot of people believe we're in challenging times, but the eternal optimist in me feels deep in my heart that the world is heading in a great direction. I see us becoming more generous as people; I see us becoming more giving and more caring. And doing this in your business, as the title of this book says, is an integral piece of shifting the paradigm of entrepreneurial success. If you want change, be the change. If you want abundance, be generous.

The world is becoming more spiritual, more awake, and evolving every day. We are growing as human beings and it is an exciting time to be alive. Things are perfect as is and getting more and more perfect every day.

So if you are committed to helping to shift the paradigm, then step up as a leader who models generosity… not only in your business, but in your life. The greatest gift is in the giving. And when you take this to heart and live this truth, you will be abundantly blessed a million times over.

CHRISTIAN MICKELSEN, author of *How To Quickly Get Started In Professional Coaching*, has been coaching for over ten years. He's been seen in Forbes, Yahoo Finance, MSN, and the Boston Globe. He served two years on the Board of Directors for the International Association of Coaching (IAC), and has created numerous support programs to help coaches become highly successful financially. For a really generous offer and subscription to his free email education system, visit www.ClientGettingEmails.com.

CHAPTER THIRTY NINE

Leading On Purpose

ANASTASIA MONTEJANO

"All is well. Everything is happening for my highest good. Out of this situation only good will come. I am safe."

~ AUTHOR UNKNOWN

MY SO-CALLED CRISIS

"You are being laid off." I put the phone down after being notified I had been laid off during the worst economic crisis in decades. The company where I worked for nearly ten years had let 900 people go. I'm one of them. The fact that I was the primary income earner for my family was starting to sink in. How in the world would I be able to support my family when I lived in a small town in northern California?

It was June of 2009. The housing market had crashed. President Obama had bailed out banking and financial institutions as the stock market was on the verge of collapse. News reports indicated that unemployment was so high there weren't jobs to apply for. All around us homes were in foreclosure because people had walked away, unable to pay their mortgages. It was grim. Still I couldn't deny the peace that prevailed and reassured me that everything would be alright.

One thought kept coming to me as I considered my next steps. What if being laid off was my opportunity to move into greater creativity and freedom? What if this so-called crisis was God's beautifully packaged gift to me? I sensed that all of my experience had brought me to this point to fulfill my highest purpose. In order to realize it I had to let go.

HUMBLE BEGINNINGS

During 28 years in corporate America, I'd held many leadership positions. The most recent was vice president and senior manager for a top investment management firm where I was responsible for the implementation of complex change initiatives in the US, Europe and Asia. I was well compensated, traveled internationally, and enjoyed opportunities to challenge and develop myself. But it wasn't always this way.

In my youth I would have been voted least likely to succeed. As the third oldest of twelve kids, there were times my family relied on food stamps, community food programs, and thrift stores to get by. At one point there were six of us sleeping in one small room! Believe me when I say I didn't live in the right neighborhood, have the right connections, or wear the right clothes. We were the family the church would come to at Christmas and Easter with donations. While I came from humble beginnings, my parents gave me something money couldn't buy. They told me I could accomplish anything I put my mind to – and I believed them.

At 19 I moved out and went to work full-time, promising myself I would do what it took to succeed. I desired to change my circumstances, but had no idea how. I stumbled through life until I was 25, when I was introduced to a book called Think and Grow Rich, by Napoleon Hill. The book's premise was that my future was only limited by my beliefs. That was when I started to examine what was possible for me and my life began to change. With small daily steps I began creating the life of my dreams. Now after working my entire career to get where I was, I was facing the fact that I could be laid off.

Are You Living Yesterday's Dream?

For nine years I had been very happy with the company, then a major reorganization occurred which impacted my role. While I enjoyed working with my team and new manager, at a deeper level I knew I was out of alignment.

I threw myself into work hoping that working harder would resolve my inner conflict. After a week of not being able to sleep, one night at 3 am I remember thinking, "Is this all there is?" What I was doing didn't fulfill me anymore. There just had to be more to life – to my purpose.

Then came the announcement of the two waves of layoffs. I knew, based on my performance record, that it was very likely that if I were in the southern California area my position would be safe; if I remained in northern California I would be laid off.

I had a choice. Choose security and move back, or make a choice based on my priorities (family, small town living, working from home), which meant leaving a multiple six figure income for an uncertain future. I chose to stay in northern California, believing that the universe is abundant and would provide what I needed, and much more.

Heeding The Call Within

I immediately began the job search process and worked at it every day for four months. While my heart wasn't into going back to a similar role, I felt I needed to bring money in as quickly as possible. The company had provided a severance package, but I knew it wouldn't last long with my current expenses. As the primary income provider for my family I needed to act quickly and do what I needed to do.

During that time I had a phone conversation with my mentor and coach, who asked me a question that turned my world on its end. She simply asked, "What would you do if you could do what you wanted to?" The words that came out of my mouth startled me. "I would launch a company focused on helping leaders discover, align with and achieve the vision and purpose for their lives."

I took a long breath to let the words settle. The deepest part of me knew exactly what I wanted. This was the first time I had come clean with myself. I only had to be willing to listen to hear what was possible for me.

These changes led me to launch Management Leadership Coaching. I did the work required to uncover my purpose and align my life's work with it. Now every day I wake up knowing I'm where I'm supposed to be, doing what I've been called to do. My life has taken on a meaning I never knew existed before this. Each day is about being open to the possibilities for my life.

This is just one example of the way my life unfolds on a daily basis. All of it came about as a result of my being willing to heed the call within me; being willing to hear and acknowledge a higher calling to my life.

WHAT IS IT YOU REALLY WANT IN LIFE?

When we're young, we're encouraged to go after our dreams – to dream big and believe that anything is possible. As we get older, somewhere along the journey we can lose the ability to dream, to believe in a bigger purpose for our lives than working to bring home a paycheck or maintaining a certain status. We may even begin to think it's too late for us. We have a mortgage to pay, kids to raise, work to do, retirement to focus on, elderly parents who rely on us. We can kid ourselves into thinking that wherever we are, it's enough for us. It may not have been what we're really passionate about, but hey, where we ended up isn't too shabby, right? I want to look you in the eyes and speak to your heart. Now you tell me. Is it enough?

What is it you really want in life? What calls to you when you quiet yourself long enough to hear? What bigger purpose are you feeling pulled towards? What's holding you back from realizing your deepest desires? Are you fulfilling your purpose where you are? Life is short – too short to waste waiting for "someday" or "later." Make today your decision point and pursue what it is you really want.

Recently both my daughters were in a local performance of the musical Cinderella. There is one poignant moment right before Cinderella leaves for the ball when she turns to her fairy godmother and says, "Nothing in my life has prepared me for this." The fairy godmother replies, "And yet everything in your life has brought you to this moment."

Your life has brought you to this very moment. Pay attention to what's showing up and be willing to go with it. It's there for a reason. Listen to what you hear in the quiet moments and respond, even if all you can do is acknowledge the call. Signs will show up to confirm you are on the path meant for you. There is no one like you on the planet. Step forward as a force of positive change. The world needs what you have to offer.

ANASTASIA MONTEJANO, ACC, PMP, helps talented, skilled professionals, managers and entrepreneurs bust through the obstacles keeping them from their full leadership, income, and career potential. As founder of Management Leadership Coaching, she uses her unique Project Management Leadership System to transform potential into powerful, effective leaders. Visit www.ManagementLeadershipCoaching.com/VIP1 to access Anastasia's #1 strategy: *What You Need to Know to Be a Highly Paid and Highly Respected Leader* – F.R.E.E. – (A value of $279.)

CHAPTER FORTY

Making Peace with Money as a Conscious Entrepreneur

KENDALL SUMMERHAWK

"What do you charge?" my client asked me. I heard the tension in her voice and knew that there was more at stake than simply setting her fees. Within a few seconds she went from excited and confident about the new offering she was launching to feeling uncertain and doubtful. What could possibly have the power to cause such a dramatic shift in her?

Money.

For conscious entrepreneurs, mentioning the word money can cause a sea of emotions to surface: everything from experiencing inner conflict over whether we're charging too much, to concern about what our peers, colleagues, family, and clients will think of us, guilt that we shouldn't be charging very much (or, if you're a successful entrepreneur, guilt that you may be making more than your loved ones or the people around you), and even annoyance and the wish that money would just "go away."

On one hand, entrepreneurs must make money in order to stay in business. On the other money represents – with very real numbers that can't be ignored – our sense of self-worth and how much we believe in the value of what we deliver. Trying to put a price on that can feel like we're selling out. Either way feels more like a cold-hearted calculation than it does a representation of our desire to serve.

At some point, most entrepreneurs will feel like they're standing at a crossroads and must choose between the path of money or the path of authenticity. What they don't realize is that they don't have to choose between the two; they can have both IF they know three simple secrets. Imagine creating lasting wealth from your business AND spiritual fulfillment, serving larger numbers of people while amassing good fortune, and increasing the value of the results you create for your clients while creating financial peace and security for yourself. In this paradigm you are not forced to choose. Instead, you're asked, "How much do you want to serve?"

Try these three simple secrets, each designed to help you charge what you're worth while expanding your ability to serve. But I must warn you: what I recommend may go against what you've learned from other well-intentioned sources. People generally mean well, but are unconsciously repeating a mindset of lack and limitation handed down to them through generations. Please keep in mind that your playing small doesn't serve anyone.

As you go through each of the secrets, notice if any feelings of resistance come up. If so, this a clear sign that you've touched on a money wound – most likely from your past – that is keeping you from achieving financial wealth and spiritual success. Rather than ignoring this feeling, ask yourself, "How is this showing up for me in my business?" I can assure you that when it comes to money, how you do one thing is how you do everything. Having the courage to transform your mindset about money will almost instantly create new opportunities and breakthroughs that will result in increasing your ability to serve others in a more powerful way, and increase the amount of money you make.

Secret #1: Stop Deciding That Your Clients "Can't Afford To Pay More"

If you're an entrepreneur who loves to help others and are always the first one your friends or family call when they need something, it's likely you frequently give up your own needs or priorities in favor of others. Pardon me for being blunt, but this is a major boundary issue. You may not feel taken advantage of, but this behavior is likely holding you back from growing your business or stepping into a higher level of success. Taken to the extreme, you may find yourself exhausted from constantly giving, without enough refueling of yourself to keep going. When it comes to money, you're usually the first person others tap for a loan, to offer a discount to a client (even before they ask), or to decide, "They can't afford me," even before you state your fees. I call this entrepreneur the "Pushover."

Contrary to your intention to "help more people," being a Pushover only serves to disempower you and the people you originally intended to help. When you keep your fees low because you've decided in advance that someone can't afford them, you rob people of an essential motivator that helps them get the results they want faster than they would have otherwise. When clients pay more, they respect you AND themselves more. They take themselves seriously and passionately devote themselves to getting the results they've longed for. So, instead of being a Pushover, align your desire to serve others with raising your fees.

Secret #2: Pay Yourself First

During my first few years in business, the idea of paying myself first sounded insane. It seemed more important to pay my mortgage, web hosting fees, and the telephone bill. Then I noticed that I always felt one step behind in how much I was making. It never seemed enough. Plus, I never felt like I had "permission" to buy things I wanted, like new clothes or furnishings for my home.

When I peeled back the curtain, I realized that by not paying myself first I was saying that I didn't count. No wonder I felt like I never had any money!

All that changed when I created my simple "Pay Yourself First" system. And yes, I created this system BEFORE I was making a higher income. Magically, not only did I have the money to pay myself, I quickly began making more than I had before without doing anything differently.

If you put off paying yourself first you're telling the world that you're not valuable. Once you begin to honor your contribution by compensating yourself first, you're going to feel valued and gain a growing sense of self-respect. Trust me, that's going to translate into more confidence marketing and growing your business.

The good news is that the amount you pay yourself doesn't matter; it's the action that counts. At a minimum, pay yourself monthly. Chose an amount and a schedule you're likely to stick with. Just be sure not to make it contingent upon getting a new client or filling a new program. Remember: you're establishing that YOU come first, no matter what.

If you're not accustomed to valuing yourself in this way, you may find "money gremlins" popping up trying to sabotage you. If this happens, simply breathe... and remind yourself this is normal. These gremlins will disappear over time as long as you stick with your "pay yourself first" mindset. If you've struggled with under-charging and under-earning, then paying yourself first is going to be a powerful step forward.

Secret #3: Don't Compromise Standing In Your Power With Money For The Sake Of Others

I believe what serves and honors you, serves and honors others. As you begin to "stand in your power" with money, those closest to you may prefer you stay exactly as you were. But holding yourself back to avoid hurting feelings doesn't do you any good, and ultimately doesn't help others either. Remember: Relationships grow when the people in them grow. Instead of compromising, be willing to stand firm in your commitment to growing your wealth.

Making more money is a blessing when used as a stepping stone on your spiritual journey. Money is symbolic of how you are growing and believing in yourself. If you've worried about what having more money will "do to you," now is the time to start trusting that having more money is part of your spiritual path. Above all, begin trusting yourself.

One of the paradigm shifts I adopted that allowed me to create a multimillion dollar business is to realize that my ability to make more money is directly aligned with the number of people I'm serving. Simply put: If you're not making much money, you're also not helping many people. It's virtually impossible to help greater numbers of people while remaining broke. When I began using money as a measurement of how many people I was serving, I realized I needed to update my business model and expand the services my business offered. As a result I created ways to help more people, which increased both my sense of spiritual fulfillment and income. This same strategy will work for you, too.

One of the tools I designed to make this easy is to ask yourself this question each day:

"As someone who makes $ _____ how do I [market my business], [handle my team], [increase my confidence, etc.]?"

The Amount Of Money You Deserve To Make Is Only Limited By The Amount You BELIEVE You're Worth

Divine source energy does not run a meter on how much money you can make. This amount is up to you. What I can promise you is that every time you create harmony and peace within you about how much money you want in your life, you'll quickly reach a new level of wealth… and experience the joy of true financial freedom.

KENDALL SUMMERHAWK is an award-winning author and the leading expert on women and money in small business. Kendall has created a heart-centered multimillion dollar coaching company focused on helping women entrepreneurs start and grow a financially and spiritually successful business. Her *How to Charge What You're Worth and Get It!®* home study course has helped thousands of women worldwide confidently increase their fees. For FREE marketing and pricing tips, visit www.KendallSummerHawk.com.

About Love Your Life Publishing, Inc.

Love Your Life Publishing, Inc. started from a casual lunch conversation at a seminar in Washington, D.C. The founders, Christine Kloser and Lynne Klippel, realized they shared a passion for helping entrepreneurs write and publish books that transformed lives and built businesses. They joked about how one of them would have to buy the other out, depending on which business grew the most rapidly.

Two years later, Christine and Lynne met at the Hershey Spa in Pennsylvania on a hunch that it was time for them to talk... about something that was yet unknown. Sitting in spa robes, eating Hershey's famous peanut butter pie, they decided not to compete, but to merge their two publishing companies and work together, blending their skill sets to bring authors more comprehensive services.

Since then, Lynne and Christine have joyfully entered into relationships with some of the top names in writing, book marketing, internet marketing, publicity, and production to create a full-service publishing company dedicated to producing great books for conscious entrepreneurs with a positive message to share with the world while growing their business.

To learn more, visit:
www.LoveYourLifePublishing.com

Free Resources

Everything You Need to Know to Get Started
Writing, Publishing and Marketing Your Book!

If you believe there's a book inside of you waiting to come out, you're in luck! After helping nearly 500 entrepreneurs become published authors, we know exactly what it takes to go from book idea to book reality... in a way that impacts you as an individual, your business, and every single reader you reach with your book.

Get your FREE Book Resource Kit now at:
www.FreeBookResources.com

What you'll receive:

E-course: Get Your Book Done Quick-Start Program
This 21-day e-course provides you with the 11 most critical steps for creating a solid foundation for success with your book. This program ensures you don't make the biggest mistakes that most authors make and guides you step-by-step to get started with your book.

Audio Program: Successful Author Secrets Bonus Pack

These five audio recordings bring you some of today's leading authors and experts in the nonfiction book world. You'll learn from John Kremer, Michael Port, Marci Schimoff, Jen Louden and us (Christine Kloser and Lynne Klippel) the inside secrets of what it really takes to succeed in writing, publishing and marketing your book as an entrepreneurial author.

Special Report: So You Want to Write a Book... Now What??

This 22-page report will open your eyes and help you understand the five step process of writing, publishing and marketing a book including all the steps you need to take to ensure the best success for your book and your business.

Get your FREE Book Resource Kit now at:

www.FreeBookResources.com

Do You Think You Should Have Been In This Book?

We know many of you reading this book thought to yourself that you should have been in it! You're not alone! Every time we publish an anthology, there are lots of entrepreneurs who read it wishing they had been one of the authors.

Well, you're in luck! We publish one anthology a year very similar to this one and we'd love to consider your chapter for our next book.

The process is simple. Just go to **www.AnthologyVIP.com** and enter your name and email address on that page.

You will be added to a special VIP list and receive the very first call for authors that we send out.

Getting published in one of our anthologies is hands-down the most powerful (and economical) way to get ready to write your own book, get tons of visibility for your business, learn the "ins and outs" of book marketing from one of the nations most well known book marketers, and be a part of something much bigger than yourself.

Your dream of getting published is closer than you think!

www.AnthologyVIP.com